ARKANSAS DAYHIKES
FOR KIDS & FAMILIES

104 EASY TRAILS IN "THE NATURAL STATE"
Second Edition

PAM ERNST
TIM ERNST
AMBER ERNST

T0168863

The design above is available as a cloth patch (actual size, $5) that is perfect for packs, shirts, caps, or just about anywhere you want to show that you hike in Arkansas! Order online at our web page www.TimErnst.com. OR you can get a patch *absolutely free* by completing the Scavenger Hunt that is included in this guidebook—see page 8 for details.

TIM ERNST PUBLISHING
JASPER, ARKANSAS

The cover photo was taken on the trail to Blanchard Springs (see p. 58 for the description). The hikers are Pam Ernst, her parents Ron & Judy Ferguson, Amber Ernst, and Amber's cousins Tyler Ferguson and Blake Ferguson. This is a very family-oriented guidebook! Photo by Tim Ernst.

Second Edition copyright © 2009, 2017, 2020 by Tim Ernst Publishing
and by Tim and Pam Ernst

All rights reserved.
No part of this book may be reproduced
in any form or by any electronic or mechanical means,
including information storage and retrieval systems,
without the permission in writing from the publisher.
Printed in the USA
Library of Congress Control Number: 2009906551
ISBN 1882906680

Other books by Tim Ernst Publishing

Arkansas Nature Lover's guidebook
Arkansas Waterfalls guidebook
Arkansas Hiking Trails guidebook
Buffalo River Hiking Trails guidebook
Ozark Highlands Trail guidebook
Ouachita Trail guidebook
Missouri Natural Wonders guidebook (Don Kurz)
Swimming Holes of the Ozarks guidebook (Glenn Wheeler)

Arkansas's Greatest Hits picture book
Arkansas Splendor picture book
Arkansas Beauty picture book
Arkansas In My Own Backyard picture book
A Rare Quality Of Light picture book
Arkansas Nightscapes picture book
Buffalo River Beauty picture book
Arkansas Autumn picture book
Arkansas Wildlife picture book
Arkansas Landscapes I & II picture books
Arkansas Waterfalls picture book
Buffalo River Dreams picture book
Arkansas Wilderness picture book
Buffalo River Wilderness picture book
Arkansas Spring picture book
Wilderness Reflections picture book
Arkansas Portfolio I, II, & III picture books

Cloudland Journal ~ Book One
The Search For Haley

Fine art prints, Pam's Pastels, Arkansas scenic calendars

Items may be ordered direct from Tim Ernst at:
Tim Ernst Publishing
Jasper, Arkansas
870–446–2382
Web Page (and secure online store): www.TimErnst.com

For my amazing daughter
Amber

May you always have the courage to explore what is around the next corner,
over the next hill, or across the river.
May you always appreciate the beauty of a sunrise and sunset,
the sound of raindrops on leaves, and the hush of a summer breeze.

When I look up I see the clouds.
When I look down I see the ground.
When I look all around I see Mother Nature sprout.
When I wake up in the morning I hear the katydids shout.
—Amber

Table of Contents

River Valley Region Trails (map page 66)

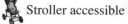 Stroller accessible   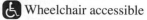 Wheelchair accessible   • On all of trail
* On only part of trail

Introduction

So, are you ready for an adventure or two? Welcome to Arkansas, The Natural State! I'm thrilled that you decided to pick up this copy of *Arkansas Dayhikes for Kids and Families* so that we can get underway and go exploring. Whether you are young or old, old in spirit or young at heart, I think you will find out something new and exciting not only about Arkansas, but about yourself as well. There is something so refreshing about going someplace new, doing and seeing things you have never done or seen before. And just plain old being out in the woods. It reminds us what life is all about....having fun!

Before we get started though, there are a few things you need to know. Please read all of the introduction and get to know your book before you head out on the trail.

About the Trails

All of the trails in this book have been hiked and approved by me. If I wasn't comfortable having Amber (my ten-year-old daughter) on the trail, I sure wasn't going to send your kids on the trail. Amber, as well as her Grandma, hiked many of these trails and had a lot of opinions on what should and shouldn't go in the book. My husband, Tim, had hiked a few of the trails for previous guidebooks, and I borrowed some of his descriptive text. He had a blast going along and discovering many of the new trails in this book with me—even this old veteran found many great and exciting places (of course, he was stopping and taking pictures all the time and I had to keep pushing him along!). All of the trails are three miles in length or less (many less then one mile). Some are more difficult than others, some are more scenic than others, but all of them have something special to offer. *Stay on maintained trails.*

And don't be fooled by the "kids" in the title of this book. These trails are for adults of all ages too who want an easier, kinder trail to hike. We have friends in their 60's, 70's and even 80's who are not only fit and energetic enough to hike nearly every day, but who seem to be enjoying life to the fullest (hum, I wonder if there is a connection there?). You are never too old to hike! And it is our hope that the grown-ups—especially grandparents—will use this guide as a road map to get the little ones outside into the wonderful world of Mother Nature. And parents, no age is too young to introduce your kids to trails—get them out there early and they will keep coming back!

We have developed a rating system called "The Dancing Hot Dogs." The more hot dogs shown above the map, the more difficult the trail. If you finish the trail you are a "REAL HOTDOGGER (or you will need to eat a lot of hotdogs to recover). This system is based relative to kids—most kids of any age should be able to do the really easy ones, but save the more difficult ones for older and more experienced kids. Most adults that hike much will be able to do all of the trails, even the three hot dog ones, although these will obviously be a little bit tougher than the one doggers.

There are dozens of easy trails throughout this book and we have made a note as to which are stroller or wheelchair accessible. Keep in mind that some stroller accessible trails are NOT wheelchair accessible, and some trails are okay for "jogger" strollers (we call them four-wheel-drive), and not for your typical push-down-the-sidewalk kind. Some of the trails are paved/accessible part of the way, but may not be so all the way. On these you can do what you can, then turn around and "stroll" back. All of that info is listed in the trail descriptions.

We have hikes that visit historic sites, boardwalks, grassy paths, wilderness hikes, wildlife viewing areas, and tough terrain. We will go to a place to dig for diamonds, explore caves, get wet by a waterfall, walk in a stream, and maybe we'll even see an alligator or two. (*What did she just say?*)

Many of the trails in this book are part of more extensive trail systems. We may have included two or three trails from a particular park, but you may find that there are several other trails in the same park. It is always best to stop by the Visitor Center for that park and get all of the additional trail brochures and info that you can. Many of the trails are special interpretive trails and have booklets that are keyed to signposts along the trail—you can pick up those booklets at the Visitor Centers as well. And as an added bonus for stopping by and talking with the great folks who operate these Visitor Centers, they will often have special programs or exhibits just for kids—they may let you pet a snake or kiss a turtle! Also many parks have Junior Naturalist or other programs that you can participate in. And, of course, we have our own little Scavenger Hunt going on where your child can win a neat "I Hike Arkansas" trail patch (free!)—more on that later.

The trails are grouped into four basic geographical areas of the state and arranged that way in this guidebook—Ozarks (northwest/northcentral), Arkansas River Valley, Southwest (Ouachitas), and Eastern. At the beginning of each section there is a regional map and list of all trails in that region (plus a list of the parks where the trails are located). There is also a statewide map showing all of the trail locations on the last page of the book—the trail numbers on all of these maps are keyed to the regional trail list on the back cover. There is a handy check box next to each trail there that you can use to keep track of how many trails you have hiked.

What to Bring

Sometimes this is the scariest part if it is your first time hiking with kids, or hiking period. What in the world do I need to *pack?!* Well, for kids it's easy. The most important thing for the kids to have on them or with them, is a WHISTLE! We'll talk about this more in the safety section, but KIDS, PACK YOUR WHISTLES! All of the trails listed can be hiked in tennis shoes or lightweight hiking boots, just make sure they are well broken in and are comfortable. There is nothing worse than hurting feet.

If your kids are comfortable with and old enough, they love to carry their own packs. These can be a simple fanny pack, or even their backpack they used for school. In it they need to carry water, a snack, a garbage bag, and according to Amber an extra pair of socks. More on that later......

As for the big people—water, snacks, first-aid kit, camera, bug spray, sunscreen, and of course, this book. According to Amber, pack the duck tape in the car also. Again, more on that later.....

The list can grow from there, to waterproof matches, toilet paper, compass, GPS unit, walking stick, etc. You name it, you can pack it. However, the trails listed in this book are rather short, so keep this in mind. We're not going on a two week backpacking trip here, just short, easy dayhikes, (but hey, maybe that's an idea for a new book).

It's always best to be prepared, so pack a rain jacket and clothing appropriate for the weather. If it's in the summer always pack a swimsuit—you just never know when the urge to take the plunge will hit you.

The hardest part for you will be to decide what to pack to keep everyone busy in the car on the way to the trailhead. Good luck with that one.

Catch the Buzz—Amber's Tips

 Throughout the book you will find a little bee in various places. This bee indicates a "Kid Tip" from Amber. These are things that she has learned or figured out along the way, and she wants to pass along her knowledge, like the duck tape tip. Some tips are a little ornery, but hey, it's all about having fun......right?

The Wise Old Owl says....

Scattered throughout the book we also have included some interesting facts and woods lore about old Mother Nature. When you see the Wise Old Owl, heads up, you just might learn something new.

Safety

Let's face it, walking down the sidewalk can be dangerous, and walking in the woods has its own set of dangers. However, walking in the woods is no more or less dangerous than walking anywhere else. The important thing is to teach your kids about issues that might come up and how to handle them.

BEFORE you head out on a hike it is extremely important for you to talk with your kids about what to do if they become separated from your group.

STAY PUT, STAY PUT, STAY PUT!!! Sit down right where they are if they have to, or if it would make them feel better move to the nearest tree and hug it. Just STAY PUT! Teach them a song to sing while they are waiting for someone to come and get them. Singing always makes me feel better (even if it sounds awful).

And now THE WHISTLE. Once they are done singing their song, and if no one has come for them yet, they need to get out their whistle. They need to blow the whistle three times (universal code for distress) and wait. Count to 20, then blow the whistle again, three times. They can then sing their song again and repeat the process.

Please teach them to only blow their whistle during emergencies. I have been on the trail plenty of times and heard a whistle, started racing toward the sound, only to find out that it was just someone playing around. Have you ever heard the story "The Boy Who Cried Wolf"? And by the way, did I mention to STAY PUT! This goes for big people as well. Even though we may think we know our way back to the group. STAY PUT!

And what about that garbage bag in their pack? The garbage bag has plenty of uses, including a rain jacket, tent, blanket, and, of course, its intended use of picking up trash. If the kids are old enough to understand, teach them to make a hole in the closed end of the garbage bag to poke their head through in case of rain (*not for little kids who could suffocate!*). During cold weather, the bag can be worn as a coat with leaves stuffed inside to help with warmth. We don't want to scare them or teach them to be on the "Survivor" show, but we do want them to be prepared if the unthinkable happens.

Snakes—okay, so they can send terror into the hearts of many, and are intriguing to others. No matter what your opinions are about snakes, stay away from them in the wild. That goes for any and all animals. We are in their living rooms now, so be respectful of them and they will be respectful of you.

Time for a good old Scavenger Hunt

We thought it would be fun to have a good old-fashioned scavenger hunt, complete with a prize, of course! Located at the end of the description on several of the trails are questions that begin with the following red text:

Scavenger Hunt ?

You can easily find the answers to each question while hiking the trail, either on an interpretive sign along the trail or in the Visitor Center located nearby.

Keep track of your answers, and once you have **ten correct answers**, simply write them down on a piece of paper and mail them to us (address is on page 2)—then we'll send you a **free patch** that declares your success! You can see the design of this patch on page one of this book. All you have to do is hike the trails and answer the questions. Not only will it be a lot of fun, but you will find yourself and your little ones learning a lot about the history of Arkansas and our wild things along the way. Good luck!

Seasons

Spring. An excellent time to hike. It's very magical here in March and April as everything comes to life. There's usually lots of water too, creating literally hundreds of waterfalls all around the state. Of course, we've got lots of wildflowers, but the trees flower wildly as well. Especially the dogwoods, redbuds and serviceberry.

Summer. It gets pretty hot and muggy towards July and August. Everyone heads to the lakes, which leaves many of the other trails deserted. There are lots of trails in this guidebook that visit lakes, and there are plenty of swimming areas too!

Fall. Each season has a certain smell to it, but none so nice as the scent of a crisp October day in the woods. Forget about all the blaze of color. Forget the deep blue sky. Forget the craft fairs. Fall just *feels* so good! Pick any trail, and you'll find a winner.

Winter. This is the longest hiking season here. Some years we have long stretches of 60–70 degree days, with brilliant sunshine. Many of the trails that run through endless tunnels of heavy forests the rest of the year, are now open to the world—with no leaves on the trees you can see deep into the hills and hollows, and out across the countryside. There are no bugs or snakes, and seldom other hikers. Of course, it can get down-right nasty too!

Weather, A Month-By-Month Guide

The weather in Arkansas is just like everywhere else—difficult to predict and constantly changing. A general rule to plan for here, or anywhere else for that matter, is to prepare for the worst weather of the season, especially rain. If it does rain, or snow, or get really hot, you'll be prepared. Here is a breakdown by month of the type of weather that you are likely to see while hiking in Arkansas. There are certainly no absolutes, because it is just as likely to be 70 degrees on Christmas Day as it is to be 0. But here are some averages.

January. This is a great month to hike. Lots of nice, clear views, and probably some ice formations too. It is one of the coldest months. Daytime highs in the 30's and 40's, with some days in the 50's and even 60's. Nighttime lows may be in the teens and twenties, but sometimes down to zero, and once in a while below zero for a short period. It may snow, but not too much, and it probably won't stay around for long. Rain is likely. But the real killer is an ice storm. They don't happen too often. When they do, the forest is just incredible!

February. Expect weather just like January. Possibly a little colder. Witch hazel bushes will pop open on sunny afternoons along the streams, and the fragrance will soothe the beast in you. I wish that they made a perfume that smelled like this.

March. Things are beginning to warm up, and get a little wetter. Daytime highs in the 50's and 60's, sometimes up into the 70's. Nighttime lows are milder, in the 30's and 40's, with a cold snap down into the 20's once in a while. Some snow, but not much. There are often long, soaking rains. Wildflowers begin to pop out. Serviceberry, wild plum and redbud trees come out and show their colors too.

April. One of the best months of the year. Daytime temps reach into the 70's and even some 80's. The mild nights are in the 40's and 50's, with still a cold snap once in a great while. Sometimes a heavy, wet snow, but this is rare. There can be some great spring thunderstorms. It's a wet month, and all of the waterfalls usually are running at full tilt. Wildflowers are everywhere. The dogwoods pop out in full bloom, and they are the most common understory tree so it is quite a sight! They will linger around some into May. The rest of the trees begin to green up too. The new growth is a brilliant kind of green that you don't see any other time.

May. Another great month, and it is the wettest month of the year. It may rain for days on end. The daytime temps reach into the upper 80's, and the nights seldom get below 60. Wild azaleas are in full bloom now. And there are still lots of wildflowers around. And waterfalls, and more waterfalls. And plenty of sunshine. The trees are all leafed out now.

June. Still good hiking weather. Less rain, and warmer temperatures. The days may reach 90, and it will drop into the 70's at night. This is the last really good month to hike for a while. The bugs start to come out, and the humidity goes up a little.

July. This is an "ify" month. It could be cool and wet, but most of the time it is pretty dry and beginning to get hot, up into the 90's, with nights still down into the 70's, or even 60's. When it does rain, it usually does so with lots of power. It's also a wonderful experience to hike in the warm rain. Put on your tennis shoes and try it sometime.

August. This is a good month to go to the beach or lake. Not a good time to be out hiking, unless you do one of the lake trails. Daytime highs can reach 100, with humidity readings to match. Sometimes it doesn't get below 80 at night. And there are lots of ticks, chiggers and other assorted bugs just waiting for you. And lots of spider webs across the trail. So if you do go hiking, remember to take that tall friend with you and let them lead (or wear a headnet).

September. This is also a good month to stay home. It is often a worse month than August. Everything is pretty much the same except that horseflies come out, and they are really a pain! Towards the end of the month, it does begin to cool off a bit. That's a good sign that better hiking is just around the corner, so you had better dust off that equipment, and maybe get into shape. Try doing some early morning hikes. You'll be surprised at who else you'll find out there on the trails with you.

October. This is the other best month of the year. The first part of it is usually still quite warm, dry and buggy. But towards the middle, the nights get cooler, down into the 50's, 40's and even 30's, and then it frosts. Yet the days are in the 70's and some 80's. By the end of the month it's crisp, clear days and nights, and in the Ozarks the forest transforms from the dull green that you have gotten used to since May, into one of the most incredible displays of color anywhere. It can be just as pretty as New England or Colorado. And out on the trails the last week of the month is always best. The bugs are pretty much gone too. Great hiking weather. The best colors in the Ouachitas don't usually happen until early November.

November. Early in the month is still kind of like October, and the best colors are happening down in the Ouachitas. Still some warm days and fall colors up in the Ozarks. But it can change quickly. The leaves die and fall off the trees. This turns everything the same color of brown, but also opens up lots of views that have been hidden since April. The days get cooler, down into the 40's and even 30's, with some nice warm days in the 60's. The nights fall into the 20's and 30's more often, and once in a while there will be a cold snap. Rain is more frequent, and once in a great while, some snow. This is the month when hunters are most active, so it is a good idea to stick to the trails in our State Parks where they don't allow hunting.

December. A good month to hike. The days are usually in the 30's and 40's, but are often in the 50's and above. The nights get cold, and can drop down to zero once in a while.

Snow is more likely, but not too much. It can rain a lot, and once in a while, some ice. When the ice begins to accumulate on some of the bluffs, it's time for a campfire, mug of hot chocolate, and marshmallows!

Mammal Tracks

There is a great deal of wildlife to be seen and heard along our trails in Arkansas. Many of the wild critters you will seldom though see simply because they are either nocturnal (only come out at night), or are very shy around people. Often the only clue that they were there will be tracks they leave behind. We have put together a few of the more common animal tracks that you are likely to see along the trail to help you with their identification (also a few not-so common ones) — see page 140, and then see how many you can find as you hike.

Thank Yous

Sometimes the words *Thank You* never seem like enough but sometimes it's all you can do. While I enjoyed every moment of exploring this wonderful state and the trails that it has to offer, every step of the way was a challenge for me. From finding the trails, learning to work the "wheelie" to measure the trails, learning what to record and how to make sure to explain it correctly, to simply writing it up. It was all a huge learning experience that I was both afraid of and enthralled by.

To keep me going and encouraging me I give my thanks to my Mom and Dad, Ron and Judy Ferguson. My best friend Sara. The best daughter and hiking partner in the world, Amber, for always saying *you can do it Mom*! And last but never least my incredible husband Tim, for giving me opportunities that I never knew existed and for simply being proud of me. And Ray, Tim's right, it really is just that simple. Tyler and Blake, thanks for putting up with your silly Aunt, and Pam, thank you for letting us borrow your kids, we had a great time. Thank you Mom, Dad and Sara for all of your editing, and Glenn, well, you lost the bet this time Mister, where's my prize?

I met so many wonderful people along the way that were willing to share all the information in the world with me. Lydia and Wanda at the Jessieville Forest Service Visitor Center — you guys are the best! Jim Warnock, Principal of Yocum Elementary School, thanks for the help with finding trails in the south. And Carolyn Royce Downs, for always thinking of us — the South isn't forgotten, just a mystery waiting to be discovered. Cane Creek was beautiful. And to the employees of the Arkansas State Parks, thanks for always taking the time to stop and teach me something new. Teachers are a true treasure, and you are indeed teachers. And to everyone else that had input in the book, thanks! James Mullins, Jon Hiser, Bob and Dawna Robinson, Ian Hope, Marlon Mowdy, April Chamblee, and Danny Gaston. Thanks guys!

And most important, Thank **you**, the reader, for taking the time to come along and explore with us. I hope that you and your children enjoy your treks as much as we have enjoyed ours. The more time our children spend in the woods, the more they will grow to love and appreciate Mother Nature, and gain a sense of respect for all wild things. Your guiding hand will lead them — and our precious natural environment that they will help protect — into the future. May your memories last a lifetime.

And remember — it's all about the *journey,* not always the destination!

Pam
Ernst

Ozarks Region Trails

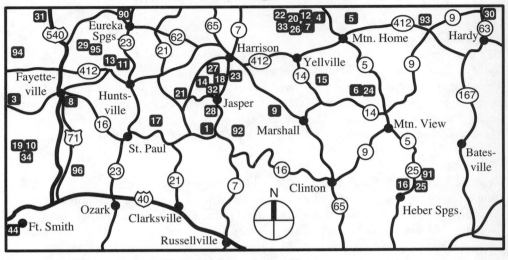

Where are the trails in this region located?

Arkansas State Parks
- Bull Shoals (4)
- Devil's Den (3)
- Hobbs State Park-Conservation Area (2)
- Lake Ft. Smith
- Mammoth Springs
- Prairie Grove Battlefield
- Withrow Springs (2)

Buffalo National River
- Buffalo Point
- Camp Orr
- Cedar Grove Picnic Area
- Hideout Hollow
- Lost Valley
- Pruitt
- Tyler Bend

Natural Heritage Commission
- Kings River Falls Natural Area

Ozark National Forest
- Alum Cove Picnic Area
- Blanchard Springs Recreation Area (2)
- Koen Interpretive Forest
- Ricketts Mountain Rock Formation

U. S. Army Corps of Engineers
- Bull Shoals Lake
- Greers Ferry Lake (3)
- Norfork Lake

Other
- Town of Beaver
- Gaston's Resort, White River (2)
- Lake SWEPCO, Gentry
- Lake Wilson, Fayetteville
- Newton Cty. Resource Council, Jasper
- Salem City Park, Salem
- Tanyard Creek Rec. Area, Bella Vista

12

Trail #	Trail Name	Hike Mileage	Difficulty*	Page #
1	Alum Cove Loop (Ozark Nat'l. Forest, Alum Cove Picnic Area)	1.1	M	43
2	Artist Point (now closed to the public)	-	-	32
3	Battlefield Loop (Prairie Grove SP)	1.0	E	26
90	Beaver Trail (Beaver)	.7	E	21
4	Big Bluff Loop (Bull Shoals SP)	1.8	M	52
5	Big Trees Loop (Norfork Lake)	.9	E+	56
6	Blanchard Springs Trail (Ozark National Forest, Blanchard)	.3	E	58
7	Bluebird Trail (Bull Shoals SP)	2.0	E	53
8	Clark Loop (Lake Wilson, Fayetteville)	2.5	D	22
9	Collier Homestead Trail (Buffalo Nat'l. River, Tyler Bend)	.9	E	46
91	Collins Creek Trail (Greers Ferry Damsite)	1.0	M	63
10	Devil's Den Loop (Devil's Den SP)	1.5	E+	30
11	Dogwood Loop (Withrow Springs SP)	.6	E+	24
12	Dogwood Nature Trail (Bull Shoals Lake)	3.0	D	51
13	Forest Trail (Withrow Springs SP)	2.1	M	24
14	Hideout Hollow Trail (Buffalo National River)	2.0	M	36
15	Indian Rockhouse Loop (Buffalo Nat'l. River, Buffalo Point)	3.0	D	48
16	Josh Park Memorial Loop (Greers Ferry Lake, Josh Park)	1.2	E	62
17	Kings River Falls Trail (Natural Heritage Commission)	1.7	E+	33
18	Koen Int. Loop (Ozark National Forest, Koen Forest)	.5	E	42
19	Lake Trail (Devil's Den SP)	1.2	E	27
20	Lakeside Loop (Bull Shoals SP)	1.0	E	50
21	Lost Valley Trail (Buffalo National River, Lost Valley)	2.7	M	34
22	Memorial Wildflower Loop (Bull Shoals SP)	.8	E	53
23	Mill Creek Loop (Buffalo National River, Pruitt)	2.2	M	40
24	Mirror Lake Loop (Ozark National Forest, Blanchard)	1.3	M+	58
25	Mossy Bluff Trail (Greers Ferry Lake, Visitor Center)	.9	M	61
26	Ozark Nature Loop (Gaston's Resort)	.9	E+	55
27	Ponds Loop (Buffalo Nat'l. River, Cedar Grove Picnic Area)	.4	E	39
92	Ricketts Mountain Rock Formation (Ozark National Forest)	.-	E	64
28	Round Top Mountain Loop (Jasper)	2.3-3.6	M+	44
93	Salem City Park Loop (Salem)	.6	E	57
29	Shaddox Hollow Loop (Hobbs State Park-Conservation Area)	1.5	M	18
30	Spring Lake Loop (Mammoth Springs SP)	.6	E	60
94	SWEPCO Eagle Watch Nature Trail (Lake SWEPCO)	.6	E	16
31	Tanyard Creek Nature Loop (Bella Vista)	1.9	E+	14
32	Triple Falls, aka Twin Falls (Buffalo National River, Camp Orr)	.5	E	38
95	Van Winkle Historic Site Trail (Hobbs SPCA)	.6	E	20
96	Warren Hollow Trail (Lake Ft. Smith SP)	1.4	M	17
33	White River Nature Loop (Gaston's Resort)	1.5	E	54
34	Yellow Rock Loop (Devil's Den SP)	2.0	M+	28

* on the kid's scale:
E—easy
M—medium
D—difficult

13

Tanyard Creek Nature Loop
1.9 miles total

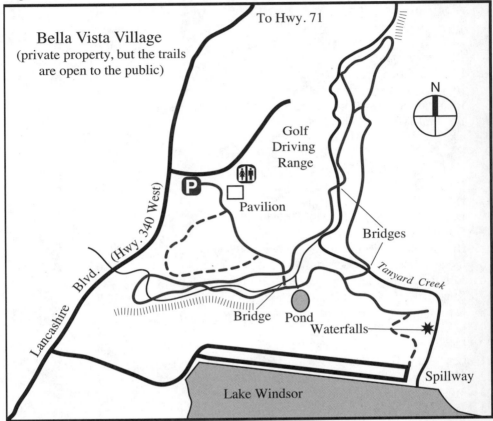

To Hwy. 71

Bella Vista Village
(private property, but the trails
are open to the public)

N

Golf
Driving
Range

(Hwy. 340 West)

P

Pavilion

Bridges

Tanyard Creek

Lancashire Blvd.

Bridge   Pond

Waterfalls

Spillway

Lake Windsor

Tanyard Creek Nature Loop. This is a wonderful trail right in the middle of Bella Vista. It was built and is maintained by volunteers, who have also posted at least 100 little signs along the way that tell all sorts of interesting details about things you will see. You can make a quick 30-minute hike to the waterfall and back, or spend half a day on this easy trail reading all of the signs. It is a "dog friendly" trail, and they even have a special dog-watering station.

To get to the trailhead from the middle of Bella Vista, head north on Hwy. 71 and take the Hwy. 340/Town Center exit, then turn left. Go just about a mile on Hwy. 340/Lancashire Blvd. and turn left—it is signed as "Tanyard Creek Recreation." Then turn right into the parking lot. There is a pavilion there, and toilets.

The trail begins next to the pavilion—TURN RIGHT and follow the paved trail out across an open field. Continue STRAIGHT ahead past a couple of intersections until you pass under a powerline, then go just a little bit farther and past the end of the pavement. At the edge of the woods you will come to a large sign that details the trail system—TURN RIGHT just before the sign and follow the little trail upstream.

The trail will pass a bridge to the left—continue STRAIGHT AHEAD and to the right, then will go over an arched bridge, and curve around to the left and come to the base of a small limestone bluff and a historical site at .4 mile, all of it is wonderful (be sure to spend some time and read all of the little signs). Follow the trail downstream along the bluff (crossing back over the little stream) until you meet up with the trail again—TURN RIGHT and cross over the creek on a bridge. The trail remains on the far side of the creek now, past neat rock formations, and comes to another trail intersection. There is a big bridge across the creek to the left that goes back to the big trail sign at .6 mile—continue STRAIGHT AHEAD at this intersection unless you are already pooped out.

There will be a small pond on your right, and soon the trail comes to another intersection—TURN RIGHT and head up the hill. This will take you to the overlook of Tanyard Creek Falls at .8 mile, a beautiful waterfall that is definitely worth the side trip! (There is also another side trail that goes up to the top of the dam and spillway, but we are not going to take it.) Once you have finished admiring the waterfall, turn around and go back to the intersection at the bottom of the hill, and TURN RIGHT there.

The trail heads on over to the main Tanyard Creek and crosses it on a large bridge. There is a nice view upstream of some cascades. (You can also TURN RIGHT just after the bridge and go upstream to a bench that has an even better view.) TURN LEFT after the bridge and head downstream. The trail joins an old roadbed here, and heads uphill just a little bit, then drops on down the other side to a point where it leaves the old roadbed at 1.1 miles—TURN LEFT here.

The next trail intersection is a short cut, but it is easy hiking ahead so continue STRAIGHT AHEAD. The trail will eventually come to the base of a small bluff and the main creek, then curve back to the left. It is an easy stroll next to the creek. At 1.4 miles the short-cut trail comes in from the left—continue STRAIGHT AHEAD.

A little ways beyond the home place the trail comes to and goes across a suspension bridge, then TURNS LEFT and continues upstream. It eventually winds back up to the large trail sign at 1.7 miles where you first entered the woods, completing your loop. TURN RIGHT and follow the paved trail back to the trailhead for a total hike of 1.9 miles.

 Wear your whistle at all times while hiking! BUT, only use it if you are really lost or hurt—never blow it just for fun.

Frog and toad eggs look alike, but toads lay their eggs in rows. Most frogs lay eggs in clumps.

SWEPCO Eagle Watch Nature Area
.6 mile lower trail round trip

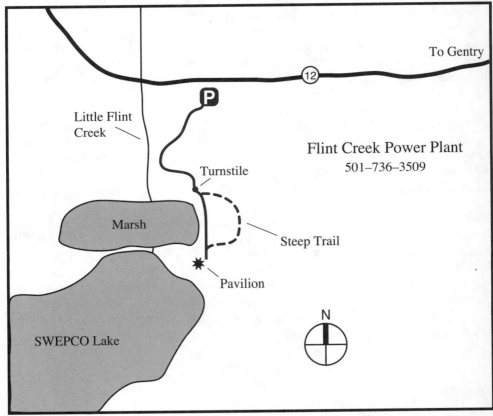

SWEPCO Eagle Watch Nature Area. If birding is a popular activity with your kids than this trail is for you. Just west of Gentry lies a birders paradise that is easy to get to and easy to hike. Strollers will have a tough time with the wood chip path so they are not really recommended. Mid-November to mid-March is the best time to watch the eagles roosting in the trees on SWEPCO Lake. The trail takes off from the parking area through a turnstile gate and crosses an open field on a wood chipped path. As you enter the woods on the other side of the field you will go through another turnstile gate and continue along a levee to a pavilion overlooking the lake. There is another trail that takes off to the left directly after the second turnstile and heads steeply up into the woods. This second trail eventually ends up at this same pavilion. To return to the parking area head back the same direction that you came in.

To get to the SWEPCO Eagle Watch Nature Area go west of Gentry on Hwy. 12 for 2 miles and parking will be on the left.

Warren Hollow Trail
1.4 mile round trip

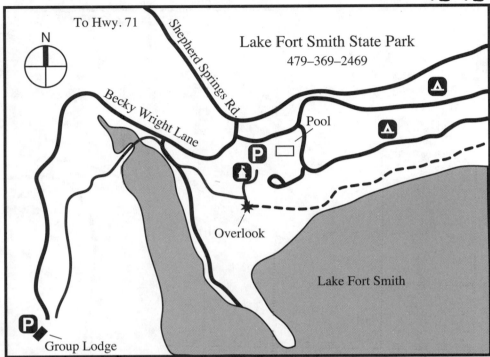

Warren Hollow Trail. The trail begins by the Ozark Highlands Trail sign to the left of the visitors center on a paved sidewalk and curves around behind the center and down a hill overlooking the lake. Before you reach the overlook you will see a sign off to the right for the Warren Hollow Trail. The trail takes off between two pine trees on gravel, over a huge rock, and you are on your way. This trail will allow some up-close time with moss covered rocks, beautiful bridges, the lake and even a waterfall if the water levels are up. When you reach the rock steps, the trail crosses a road and heads to the right. Follow the bright green blazes that are painted on the road. This is a great opportunity to talk with your kids about blazes and what they mean. As you approach Becky Wright Lane the trail turns to the left and crosses over a levee—watch for turtles basking on the logs. On the other side of the levee cross the road and a bridge and head back into the woods. After heading uphill a ways you will come to a bridge that crosses over a stream with a possible waterfall. A second road is crossed shortly after this bridge. Watch for the blazes. You will come to the end of Warren Hollow Trail when you emerge from the woods at a basketball court and parking area. Turn around and go back the same way you came.

To get to Lake Ft. Smith State Park take Exit 34 between Fayetteville and Ft. Smith. Turn towards Hwy. 71. There are very few signs here for the state park. You will be on Hwy 248 East. After a mile up hill you will intersect with Hwy. 71 and will see a sign for Lake Ft. Smith State Park, turn left. At 4.2 miles turn right onto Shepherd Springs Road. At 2.1 miles turn right onto Becky Wright Lane into the visitors center. There is camping, fishing, boating, hiking and a beautiful swimming pool to be enjoyed in the immediate area, so plan to spend the day.

Shaddox Hollow Loop
1.5 miles total

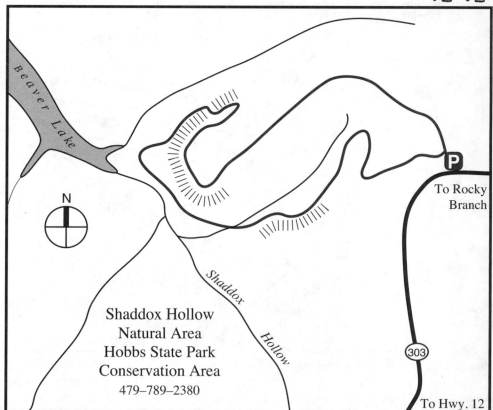

To Rocky Branch

N

Beaver Lake

Shaddox Hollow

Shaddox Hollow
Natural Area
Hobbs State Park
Conservation Area
479–789–2380

303

To Hwy. 12

Shaddox Hollow Loop. This is a short, popular loop that visits Shaddox Hollow Natural Area, which is jointly managed by the Natural Heritage Commission and Arkansas State Parks. It is part of the Hobbs Park—Conservation Area, and is located along the shores of Beaver Lake in NW Arkansas near Rocky Branch. Besides lots of bluffs and streamsides, this area contains a wide variety of fauna and flora, and is frequented by school science classes and used as a training aid. The scenery is pretty darn nice too! The trail was built as a tribute to Virginia Allred, a longtime resident of the area and well–known conservationist.

To get to the trail, take Hwy. 12 east out of Rogers, past Beaver Lake, turn north on Hwy. 303 (this is the turn off to Rocky Branch) and go about one mile—the parking lot is on the left. There is lots of room to park. The trail begins at the carved wood sign, down a set of steps. We'll hike this trail in a counterclockwise direction, so TURN RIGHT at the sign. The trail takes off fairly level and swings around the head of a hollow to the left. It heads down the middle of a ridgetop. All along here there is a thick cover of huckleberry, which is actually wild blueberry. They ripen in early summer.

It continues along the ridgetop, remaining level. During leaf–off there are some pretty nice views through here. As the trail gets on out to the end of the ridge, it swings to the left, then to the right as it drops on down the hill at .5 mile. There is a stunning view out over Beaver Lake here. (This is the turn around point if you don't want to do the whole trail—once you head down the hill, you'll have to climb back out, so you may want to go back the easy way.) It curves back to the right as it continues to drop. You'll notice that much of the tread and the hillside look like gravel—a natural pile! As the trail comes up on a small ravine, it switchbacks to the left and continues on down the hill.

There is an interesting "hole" just off to the left—this is a sink hole, which is actually a place where water comes gushing into some cave system deep below. Just beyond, the trail makes its way down a set of steps through the bluffline at .7 mile, then levels out and runs along the base—all of this area is wonderful. You can get up close to the bluff and see lots of neat stuff. If you look close, you'll see places where critters live! The trail swings around the bluff to the left, then leaves the bluff area TO THE RIGHT, and heads down hill.

As it curves back to the left there is a spur trail that goes off to the right to the shore of the lake. The main trail goes over and comes alongside a wonderful little stream, and follows it upstream. This area along the stream is another terrific spot to stay awhile. There is a short footbridge over a side drainage, and the trail continues on the level near the stream. Here and there you'll pass a few large trees. And of course in the springtime, there are lots and lots of wildflowers along the way. Eventually the trail swings back to the left and comes to a larger bridge at .9 mile. When the water is running this is a great spot to sit and dangle your feet off of.

Past the bridge the trail works its way uphill just a tad and into a real neat little ravine, coming to an overhanging bluff. It's the largest bluff along the trail. The tread gets kind of narrow just beyond, as it goes across the steep hillside. All through this section you can look down on the creek. Eventually the hillside levels out just a bit, and the trail turns to the right, goes up another small drainage a few feet, and crosses a stream just below a waterfall. It begins to head uphill some, as it goes across the nose of a ridge.

The hillside gets pretty steep again as the trail swings to the right into a small ravine. This is a neat little stream crossing—everything is covered with moss, and there is a waterfall upstream. From here the trail heads uphill again, and swings wide around the edge of a hillside, and turns up to the right. It gets a little steep at times. Just take your time. The trail curves back to the right across the hillside, then back to the left. It's not quite as steep through here. A little more uphill, then the trail ends back at the parking lot.

Be sure to stop by the Hobbs State Park Visitor Center where you'll find all kinds of neat stuff and can talk with a ranger!

 If you see branches on the trail when you hike, kick them off as you walk by. It will help keep the trail clean.

The green treeforg is nicknamed the "rain frog" because it often sings just before and during a thunderstorm.

Van Winkle Historic Site
.6 mile round trip

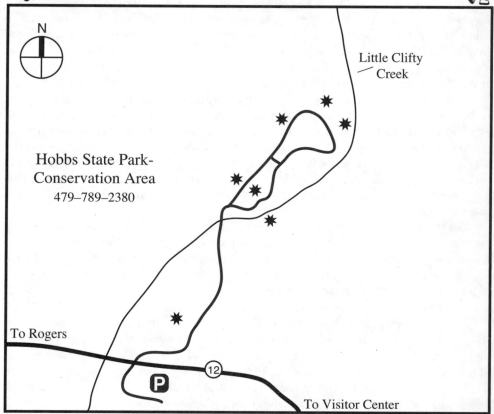

N

Little Clifty
Creek

Hobbs State Park-
Conservation Area
479–789–2380

To Rogers

12

P

To Visitor Center

Van Winkle Historic Site. The Historic Van Winkle Trail is located within the Hobbs State Park-Conservation Area and is a great little trail for the little ones that barely have their footing. With wide paths part paved and part gravel, they can run to their hearts content. If their not quite to the walking stage yet the trail is wheelchair and stroller accessible. Dogs are allowed on this trail but they must be on a leash at all times. Restrooms are available at the trailhead.

The trail winds through the historic Van Winkle industrial mill complex with views of where the slaves quarters, antebellum home, spring house and the old mill once stood. From the trailhead follow the paved path curving to the right and going under the highway through a tunnel. There are informational signs along the way to provide a great history lesson for everyone. The trail follows along Clifty Creek and soon crosses over the creek on a bridge. Here the trail splits to form a loop. Heading to the right you will find the remnants of the Van Winkle's old spring house and a crystal clear creek with a pretty bluff. The trail curves around passing the old mill, the house, the old garden area and several other historical remnants.

Be sure to visit the new and fantastic Visitor Center located 1.4 miles east of the trail. The Visitor Center is open daily from 8-5 and has some wonderful educational interactive exhibits. The park is located 10 miles east of Rogers on Hwy. 12.

Beaver Trail
.7 mile round trip

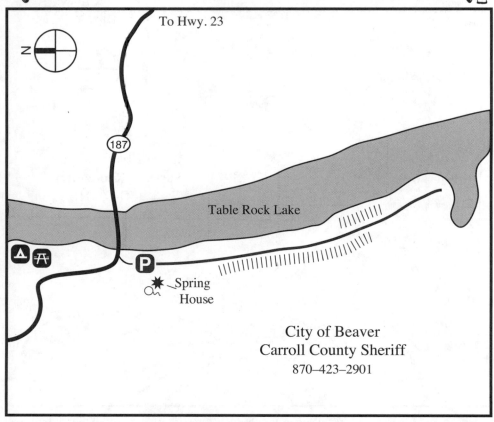

To Hwy. 23

N

187

Table Rock Lake

P

Spring
House

City of Beaver
Carroll County Sheriff
870–423–2901

City of Beaver Trail. To get to the town of Beaver, Arkansas and this wonderful little hike take Hwy 23 North out of Eureka Springs for 5.8 miles and turn left onto Hwy. 187. Go 2.7 miles, crossing over the wooden suspension bridge to the trailhead. Immediately after you cross the bridge turn left into the parking area. No camping, no fires, no fireworks allowed. Fishing is allowed as well as pets on a leash.

The trail takes off directly after the sign and follows along Table Rock Lake on an old railroad bed. Be sure to check out the stone Beaver Spring House at the parking area. This hike is good for jogger strollers and is an easy stroll for everyone. With a wide path, the lake on the left and a beautiful bluff on the right, this stroll is so relaxing. At about .3 of a mile you will come to the remains of an old train trestle. This is the end of the trail so just turn around and head back the way you came. There are a few places along the way that the kids will have an opportunity to get down to the waters edge. Across the street from the parking area is Table Rock Lake State park, so plan to spend the day.

Scavenger Hunt ? What year was the stone Beaver Spring House built?

Clark Loop
2.5 miles total

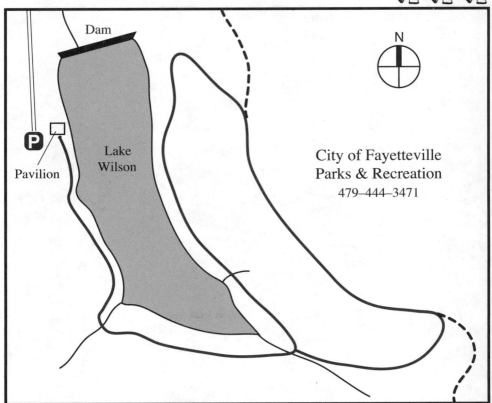

Dam

N

P

Pavilion

Lake
Wilson

City of Fayetteville
Parks & Recreation
479–444–3471

Clark Loop. Located at Lake Wilson is a hidden treasure of the city of Fayetteville. If adventure is what you want, well, the drive out to Lake Wilson is an adventure in itself. To get to Lake Wilson from the Junction of Hwy. 265/ Crossover Rd. and Hwy. 16 in Fayetteville, go west .5 mile to Happy Hollow Rd., turn left. Go another .5 mile to a stop light. Continue through the stop light (Hwy. 16 is now 15th street), another .5 mile and turn left on Morningside Drive. Morningside is also known as Hwy. 156 and City Lake Rd. On Hwy. 156 go 1.9 miles to Wilson Hollow Rd. and turn left. If you reach gravel in .2 mile you are on the right road. After you turn left on Wilson Hollow Rd., you will come to a one lane bridge at .9 mile, do not cross this if the water is high, and in fact if the water is high this entire area will be closed. You will come to an intersection, turn left here, this will be the first sign directing you to Lake Wilson that you will see. Continue straight ahead until you reach the pavilion.

The hike begins on regular trail directly to the right of the pavilion. There is not a sign there, just a post. DO NOT START THROUGH THE GATE. The first part of this trail is fairly level and walks along the shores of Lake Wilson. There is no swimming here or restrooms. There are blazes along the way. The trail curves around and down into a creek bed at .3 mile. If the creek is running this will be a wet crossing. Cross the creek and go up the other side, curve to the left and the trail gets pretty rocky through here, but it is beautiful. Off to your left is Lake Wilson and during leaf-off the views will be spectacular. At .4 mile the trail curves up to the right and heads away from the lake. At .5 mile you will come to a little creek and follow it upstream a little ways before crossing. Another wet crossing if the creek is running.

You will see a green sign on the other side of the creek—TURN RIGHT at the sign and begin the loop portion of the hike. Continue upstream a ways and at .6 mile curve to the left and head uphill. There is a neat bluff up to your left that you will meet and wind your way through at .7 mile. NEAT SPOT!!! The trail curves to the left and makes its way through the bluff. At .8 mile you will come to an old forest service road, continue STRAIGHT ahead. You are on the level road now, YEAH! At 1.3 miles the trail curves to the left, goes down slightly, your intersection is coming up, TURN LEFT. WATCH for this turn, it can slip by you. When you TURN LEFT you will be following a creek down the hillside. Good stuff is coming! If the creek is running you will soon be standing next to a waterfall area. Curve right and head down through the bluff line. Once through the bluff line look back up to your left, the view is GREAT! The trail meanders through the woods curving left and right and heading mostly downhill. Views of the lake are off to your left. The trail takes a sharp turn to your left at 1.5 miles. At 1.7 miles you will arrive back down on the shores of Lake Wilson and in the early morning you can see the fish flopping. At 1.9 miles you will pass by a really neat leaning tree and a huge rock standing on its side, shortly after, the trail curves to the right and heads downhill. The original intersection arrives at 2.0 miles, continue STRAIGHT ahead across the creek to get back to the parking area.

Scavenger Hunt ? Who was this trail named for?

Purple paint blazes on a tree usually mean there is private property behind the tree—don't go there.

Chipmunks do not go into hibernation during the winter. They go into states of "torpor" or extended rest.

Forest Trail
2.1 miles round trip

Dogwood Loop
.6 mile total

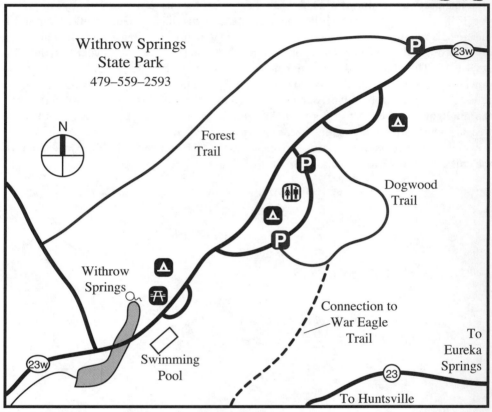

Forest Trail. This one is great for beginners, and perfect for that "first trip into the woods" experience. There aren't any real spectacular features, such as bluffs, waterfalls, or caves, but the trail is nice and wide, fairly flat except for at the beginning, and is just a nice easy hike. And for those of you who love Dogwood Trees, well, it doesn't get much better than this.

To get to Withrow Springs State Park from Huntsville go north five miles on Hwy. 23 to the park, or take Hwy. 23 south from Eureka Springs for 20 miles. There is a swimming pool, campgrounds and great picnic places at this park, so plan to spend the day or the entire weekend.

From the Visitor Center continue straight ahead for 1.1 mile. The trailhead is on the left with a fabulous parking area. Head up the steps and into the forest.

You may be saying to yourself, hey these crazy people sent me on this trail. Don't worry, it only goes up for a mere 620 feet. Then it is level the rest of the way (and on the way back, all of that uphill will be down!). You might try the marching game to get the kids up this steep section. Just like in the army, have them march—make up a song to go along with it all and you will be to the top in no time.

At .3 mile the trail curves to the left. There are huge dogwood trees through here so springtime is prime time to hike this trail. The trail will come to a paved road at a little over a mile, just turn around and head back the direction you came from.

At just over 2 miles the hike can be a little long for really young kids. But hey, since it is not a loop trail you can turn around and head back anytime, it's downhill the rest of the way.

Dogwood Loop. Dogwoods and wildflowers are the name of the game on this trail. To get to Withrow Springs State Park from Huntsville go north 5 miles on Hwy. 23 to the park, or take Hwy. 23 south from Eureka Springs for 20 miles. There is a swimming pool, campgrounds and great picnic places at this park, so plan to spend the day or the entire weekend.

Once you enter the park and pass the Visitor Center continue STRAIGHT ahead for .5 mile. After you pass Keith Ham Pavilion take the next gravel pull-off on your right. The Dogwood Trail starts immediately off to your right across from campsite 14 and heads up into the woods. There are restrooms located at this pull-off area.

The trail starts out fairly steep, just take your time and enjoy the amazing ferns and in the spring the abundance of trillium. At about .1 mile the trail curves back to the right and shortly after that the trail curves back to the left. If you look up to your right there is a bench. CONTINUE LEFT, look for the blazes. After you make this curve the trail levels out. The trail meanders through a beautiful hardwood forest and is named for the many dogwoods that you will find along the way. At .4 mile the trail starts to head downhill. Shortly after that you will curve to the left, then back to the right and head downhill some more. At .5 mile the trail heads down hill pretty steeply and you will find yourself back at the road. Once you get to the road, TURN LEFT to return to your car.

If you get separated from your group, STAY CALM, STAY PUT (hug a tree), and sing a song. They will come find you before too long. While you are waiting, see how many different bugs you can count.

A red trillium wildflower looks pretty but smells like rotten meat. This odor draws flies which pollinate the plant.

Battlefield Loop
1.0 mile total

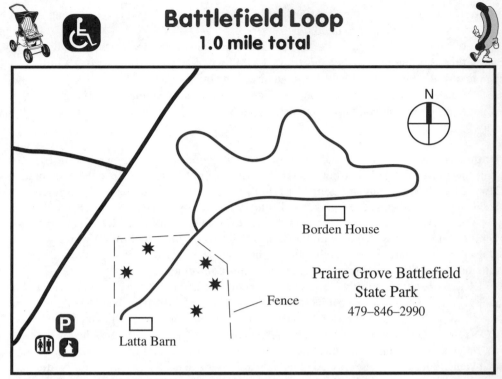

N

Borden House

Praire Grove Battlefield
State Park
479–846–2990

Fence

Latta Barn

Battlefield Loop. Prairie Grove Battlefield State Park is located within a short distance from Fayetteville. This is a wonderful State Park with a playground, plenty of facilities, beautiful scenery and is a complete educational experience. The Battlefield Trail is paved the entire way and even though it does have somewhat of a hill on the way out, it is wheelchair and stroller accessible.

To get to the park from Fayetteville, travel west on Hwy. 62 for 8.8 miles. The park is located on the eastern edge of the town of Prairie Grove. Admission is free. After you have entered the park the Visitor Center is located on your left. We will park there to begin our hike. We recommend that you step inside the Visitor Center and take a look around. There is a short program that will help you understand the battle and the sites that you are about to hike through. Pick up a trail brochure at the Center that will tell stories and point out interesting details along the way.

From the parking area at the Visitor Center you will TURN RIGHT and walk along a stone wall, following it as it curves around to your left. As you curve to the left you will see a building on your right called the Latta Barn (restrooms are available here). Directly after the Latta Barn is a large sign for the Battlefield Trail.

The trail is paved through here but you are more than welcome to get off of the trail to take a closer look at these historic buildings. Shortly after passing the old school house you will come to a fence and you will see a fork in the trail. TURN RIGHT. Watch out for the squirrels....they are feisty.

You will come to a house called the Borden House. Continue STRAIGHT ahead. The trail curves around to your left and heads downhill. You will head through an open field, curve to the left and head back uphill. There are benches along the way to rest. Once to the top of the hill you will arrive back at the intersection, TURN RIGHT to get back to your car.

Scavenger Hunt ? Why is a "dog trot" house called a "dog trot" house?

Lake Trail
1.2 miles round trip

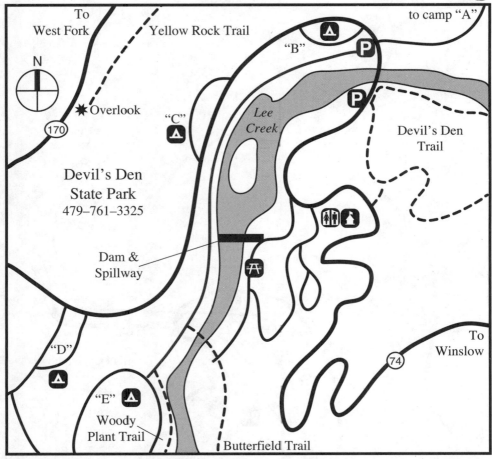

To West Fork

Yellow Rock Trail

"B"

to camp "A"

N

Overlook

170

"C"

Lee Creek

Devil's Den Trail

Devil's Den State Park
479–761–3325

Dam & Spillway

"D"

"E"

Woody Plant Trail

74

To Winslow

Butterfield Trail

Lake Trail. If you want to see some unique things in Mother Nature, then travel to Devil's Den State Park. Located just south of Fayetteville, it offers a wonderful retreat from city life. To get there from Fayetteville, drive 8 miles south on I-540. Take State Hwy. 170 at West Fork (Exit #53) 17 miles to the park; or, from I-540 near Winslow, take State Hwy. 74 (Exit #54) seven miles west to the park. Park just north of the bridge across Lee Creek.

The trail begins from the parking area and is fairly level following the lake shore. Swimming is not allowed, but they do have paddle boats for rent (in season). At .3 mile you will arrive at the dam and spillway of Lee Creek that was built by the Civilian Conservation Corps back in the 1930's. Beautiful area. Do not go across the dam, continue STRAIGHT ahead and to your right. At .4 mile you will come to a huge suspension bridge. If you would like a longer hike go across here and continue around to the parking area for a total of about 1.5 miles, otherwise continue STRAIGHT ahead. At .6 mile you will come to an intersection and this concludes the Lake Trail. TURN AROUND and head back the way you came for a total hike of 1.2 miles.

There are lots of great trails in this park (two more follow here)—be sure to stop in at the Visitor Center for all of the details.

Yellow Rock Loop
2.0 miles round trip

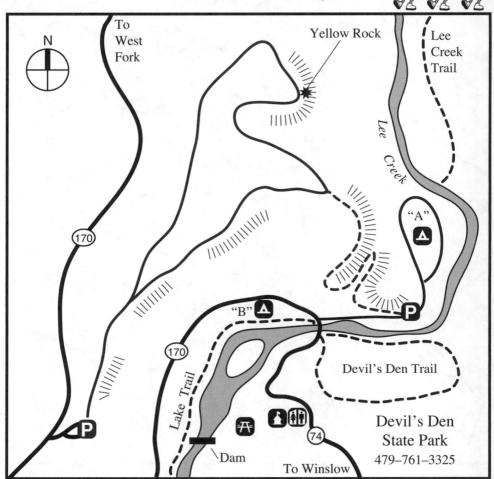

Yellow Rock Loop. Here is another of the three great trails we include in this guidebook from Devil's Den State Park. It can get a little tough for the tiny tots, so either take it easy, or reserve this one for older kids. Spectacular views! To get to the park, drive eight miles south of Fayetteville on I-540. Take State Hwy. 170 at West Fork (Exit #53) 17 miles to the park; or, from I-540 near Winslow, take State Hwy. 74 (Exit #54) seven miles west to the park. The Yellow Rock Trailhead is located just off of Hwy. 170 at the north end of the park on the big hill looking down into the Lee Creek Valley. The pull-off area is marked as a scenic overlook.

From the parking area you will go down the steps to the scenic overlook building and TURN LEFT, you will begin by staying fairly level, winding through the forest. After crossing over two bridges you will come to an intersection, TURN LEFT. This trail is a loop trail so you'll see this intersection again. You'll continue by going up and curving to the right. You will see a horse trail take off to your left, but you want to continue STRAIGHT AHEAD. There is an area directly after the horse trail that will be especially beautiful when it is wet—waterfalls! Be careful though, if it is real wet, this will be a wet crossing for you.

Directly after the stream the trail comes to an intersection, TURN RIGHT and head towards Yellow Rock. After you TURN RIGHT you will head down the hillside, curve to the right and head steeply down the hillside. Take your time through here. Once you are down the hillside you will come to a bluff and this is the official Yellow Rock area. There are no guard railings through here so watch the kids. There is plenty of room through here for them to stay away from the edge and the view is nothing short of spectacular. Great place for a snack. The "yellow" in Yellow Rock comes from the color of iron oxide stains on the sandstone bluff.

Continuing on, the trail takes out to the left of Yellow Rock up what looks like a gully. At 1.3 miles you will come to another intersection, TURN RIGHT and head uphill, a *lot* uphill. (If you turned left the other part of the trail winds down through a number of bluffs and rock formations to the lower trailhead on the road to Camp Area A.) Take your time, march if you have to. The trail curves to the left and levels out, WAHOO!!!! At 1.5 miles you will come to a slab of rock that is called Carpet Rock. It's neat! Amber calls them Tic-Tac-Toe rocks—you'll understand why when you see them. You'll come to the original intersection and continue STRAIGHT ahead back toward the bridge and original parking area.

 An easy way to get yourself up a steep hill......march!

Skunks love to eat bumblebees.

29

Devil's Den Loop
1.5 miles total

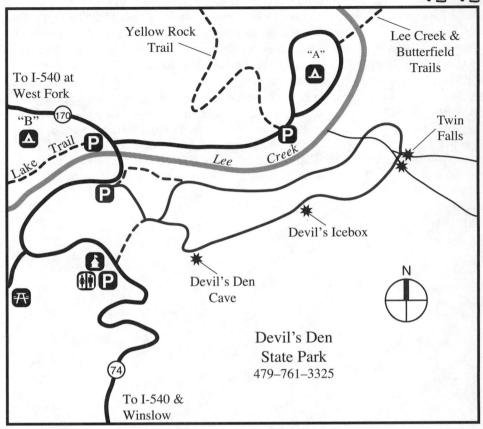

*CAVE CLOSURE NOTICE. Some caves may be closed to all entry to help stop the spread of a disease that has killed millions of bats in the United States. Obey posted signs!

Devil's Den Loop. If you like caves be sure to pack the flashlights for this one. Even if you're not into caves (which I am not), this trail is WONDERFUL! This is one of the most popular trails in the park, indeed in all of Arkansas—with all of the neat things along the way, you will quickly see why. To get to the park from Fayetteville, take I–540 south to State Hwy. 170 at West Fork (Exit #53), then 17 miles to the park; or, from I-540 near Winslow, take Hwy. 74 (Exit #54) then seven miles west to the park. The main trailhead is located just south of the big bridge across Lee Creek—lots of parking there! You can also park and begin your hike from the Visitor Center if you like. Be sure to stop in at the Visitor Center to pick up a brochure. There are numbered posts along the trail and there is more info in the brochure that is keyed to those numbers.

The trail takes off to the left side of the main parking area and heads up a set of steps. You'll come to an intersection once you get to the top of this little hill, TURN LEFT. Shortly after, you will see a trail heading off to your left, continue STRAIGHT ahead. The main trail curves to the right, heads uphill, then switchbacks to the left. The cave entrance isn't far away, and is easy to spot.

The entrance is actually just a large crack in the rock, and it is an easy trip down into the cave, although it is kind of narrow. Experienced explorers only should venture very far inside (it goes back in more than 500 feet), but others can go far enough to get completely away from any outside light–then pause for a moment and have everyone turn their lights off—you'll get to experience TOTAL DARKNESS!

Once back outside, continue along the trail past the cave entrance and you will come to an area that has a deep crack in the rocks. Watch your kids in this area. At the end of the crack in the rock you will curve to the right and head down some steps and now you are looking at the Devil's Icebox. It's a wonderful place to rest in the summer, and you can feel the cool air from deep inside the mountain rising as the cave system below breaths.

The trail curves around and comes up next to a bluff that has seen many years of erosion. At .4 mile you will come to an intersection with an arrow pointing to the right, I know, it looks like there is no trail there and is just a big jumble of rocks, but trust me, go on over and have a look, the trail is indeed there. TURN RIGHT.

The trail follows along at the bottom of a bluff and comes to a pair of waterfalls known as Twin Falls. When the falls are running you are likely to get sprayed since the trail goes behind the first waterfall. Also, this is a great picture opportunity as there is a bridge that goes across the stream at the bottom of the second falls.

There are a lot of steps immediately past the falls area, so be sure to stay on the trail. At the bottom of the steps after the wooden bridge is a great place to stop and have a snack and watch the waterfalls above. At Cold Springs the trail curves to the left and up a set of steps and across a bridge. Follow the trail along past the old Donald Homestead. At the next intersection, TURN LEFT. This will take you back to the original intersection where you will TURN RIGHT to return to the parking area.

Bats can eat their own weight in mosquitoes each day and are great friends to have around. Watch them fly—every time they make an erratic direction change they are catching a bug!

When you see a double blaze on a tree, PAY ATTENTION—the trail is getting ready to turn.

A gray squirrel's top front teeth grow about six inches a year, so it has to chew to keep them worn down.

Artist Point Trail
Closed to the public

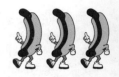

Artist Point Trail. This trail has been closed by the land owner due to vandalism and is no longer open to the public. *Please be respectful* of all the surroundings as you hike and always practice a good LEAVE NO TRACE ethic—

LEAVE nothing but footprints.
TAKE nothing but pictures.
KILL nothing but time.

THANK YOU!!!

Kings River Falls Trail
1.7 miles round trip

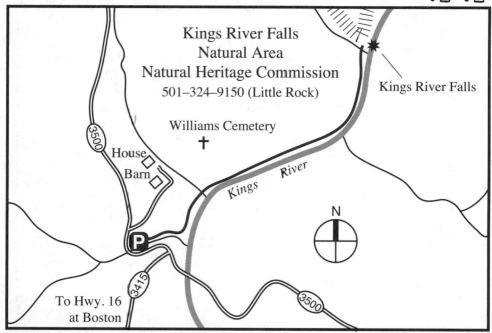

Kings River Falls
Natural Area
Natural Heritage Commission
501–324–9150 (Little Rock)

Kings River Falls

Williams Cemetery
✝

House
Barn

Kings River

3500

N

P

To Hwy. 16
at Boston

3415

3500

Kings River Falls Trail. This short, easy to hike trail will take you to the waterfall that is pictured on the cover of our *Arkansas Hiking Trails* guidebook. The spot is an "Arkansas Natural Area," and is administered by the Natural Heritage Commission. Many people find this trail difficult to get to, but it's real easy if you follow these directions: From the used–to–be community of Boston on Hwy. 16 (between Fallsville and St. Paul), go north on County Road #3175 (gravel) for two miles, then turn right as the road forks on CR#3415. Stay on this road 2.4 miles (it gets rough in a spot or two, but don't give up), until you come to a "T" intersection, and turn left on CR#3500. Go a couple of hundred yards and park at the trailhead, which is located at the bridge that goes across Mitchell Branch. (This trailhead was built in 2009—the old one next to the crumbling barn is no longer there.)

This is an easy, level trail (perfect for kids) that is marked with blue blazes. The trail begins at the parking area and heads downstream along the top of a small levy, and follows in between the creek (on the right) and hay field/fenceline (on the left). It comes alongside the Kings River and follows the field to the left, then crosses a small stream.There is an old rock wall part of the way that defines a hay field. Besides tons of wildflowers that carpet the area in the spring, there are lots of wild azaleas around too. Stay next to the river, and you'll eventually come to the Natural Area boundary sign—the wonderful waterfall and pool are just beyond at .6 mile. There is a small side creek coming in from the left that has some nice waterfalls once in a while. The immediate area of the big falls was once used as a grist mill site—can you spot the marks carved into the stone?

This area is pretty nice all around—plan to spend some time here! The swimming is a little cold, but after the hike in, it is always a treat. To return to the trailhead, head back upstream the way that you came in.

Lost Valley Trail
2.7 miles round trip

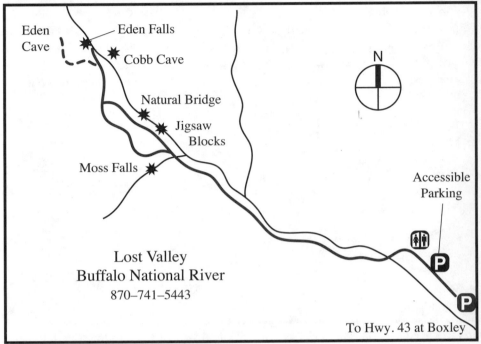

Lost Valley Trail. This little area is one of the special places in the world, and is one of Amber's favorite trails in the entire state. This popular trail will seem short, and for the most part, very easy to hike. Although the last section of trail does get pretty steep as it climbs up to a cave—which reminds me—be sure to bring a flashlight (one for each hiker) if you wish to go into the cave.

The trail is located at Buffalo National River, at the Lost Valley Trailhead. To get there, turn off of Hwy. 43 between Boxley and Ponca at the Lost Valley sign, and follow this road to a giant gravel parking lot. *NO dogs are allowed on the trail.*

The trail begins at the far end of the parking area and is level, going past an accessible parking area, pavillion, restrooms, and a small picnic area. There may or may not be a foot-bridge across Clark Creek—if there is a bridge, cross it to continue on the trail (if no bridge, you may have to wade the creek but the trail will be obvious). This is the creek that the trail will follow up into its headwaters.

The first half-mile or so is on a wide, level trail, easy for strollers and somewhat for wheelchairs, although wheelchairs must stop there and strollers would have a tough time of it. It's a nice stroll that passes some large trees, including sweet gums, cedars, and some giant beeches. The creek is a typical babbling brook, with lots of smooth rocks for a floor. It does dry up once in a while though—springtime is the greatest here!

The trail forks at .9 mile and becomes narrow and rocky—TURN RIGHT (you will return on the trail that comes down the hill on the left). The trail runs along the creek to some huge stone blocks. These are called "Jig Saw Blocks," and you can probably figure out why. It looks like they fell off of the bluff just behind them—that would have been interesting! Just beyond, the trail comes to the Natural Bridge on the right. All of this area is simply

34

breathtaking. When the water is running good, this is a magical little spot. When it's almost dry, you can actually hike through the bluff, and come out on the other side upstream.

Continue on up the trail (bear right at the next two forks), and you'll find yourself standing at the base of a 200–foot bluff, and Cob Cave at 1.3 miles. This is the giant overhang that you can hike back into. Plan to spend some time exploring here. This is also a great place for refueling before your hike back. At the far end of this spot is Eden Falls, which is a spectacular waterfall. The falls come out of Eden Falls Cave. There are lots of mosses, ferns and other lush stuff around the base of these falls.

No matter what time of year you are here, you're sure to find something that interests you. Spring is great of course. But so is fall, with all the colored leaves. And even the dead of winter is nice. One hint for popular times—come during the week to avoid the crowds!

There is a trail that leads up to the cave. NOT recommended for the young kids but we'll give the directions just in case you have some real explorers on your hands. To get to the cave, go back down the trail to the first intersection that you come to, TURN RIGHT, and follow the trail up the hill. It's a short but steep climb, and the view back behind gets better with every step. The trail ends at the cave at 1.4 miles—use some caution here, 'cause it's pretty narrow and it's a long drop! Eden Falls Cave isn't very large or long, but it does have Clark Creek flowing out of it, which makes it special indeed. This is of course what makes Eden Falls that we just saw from below. It's not an easy crawl to get back into the cave. But if or when you get in, you'll be rewarded, because the creek also forms a waterfall inside the cave—it's about 35 feet tall.

To get back to the campground, just head back the same way that you came in, only bear right at all intersections (you'll hike a short stretch of trail that you didn't hike on the way in, and pass "moss falls" on the right). Soon you'll be back at the lower trail intersection, and from there it's a nice level stroll home, making a total hike of 2.7 miles.

This entire trail is simply magical, around every turn is something new and exciting. Take the family on this hike first and they will be hooked on hiking forever.

Scavenger Hunt ? **How many man-made bridges do you cross on this trail?**

Pack extra socks—use them if your socks get wet, or on hot days dip your socks in water and place them around your neck to help you cool off.

Ants have an average life span of 8 years.

Hideout Hollow Trail
2.0 miles round trip

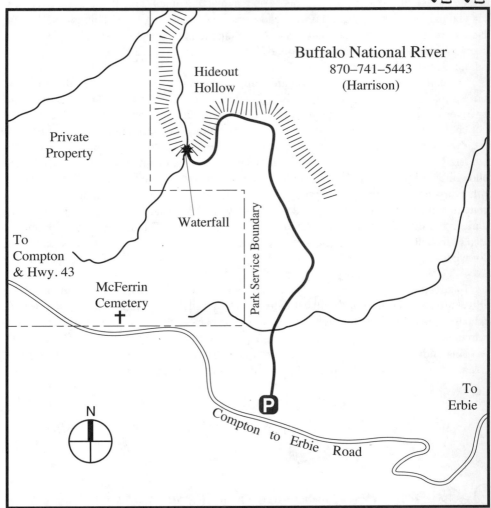

Buffalo National River
870–741–5443
(Harrison)

Hideout
Hollow

Private
Property

Waterfall

To
Compton
& Hwy. 43

Park Service Boundary

McFerrin
Cemetery
✝

To
Erbie

P

N

Compton to Erbie Road

Hideout Hollow Trail. This is a wonderful little trail that takes you into a large bluff and waterfall area. It is often overlooked by hikers, since it is one of the lesser-known trails in the Buffalo National River trails system—you won't see many other folks here. The hike is pretty easy, with only a few ups and downs. Many of the oak trees have been dying due to red oak borer beetles, so watch out for dead limbs that drop unexpectedly. Camping is allowed but there are no facilities. *No dogs are allowed on the trail.*

To get to the trailhead, which is called the Schermerhorn Trailhead, go north out of the town of Ponca on Hwy. 43 for 8.3 miles, turn right at Compton and go 3.5 miles. You'll see the trailhead on the left just after you pass the National Park Service Boundary sign. (The road continues down the hill, very rough at times, and goes to the Cecil Cove Trailhead, and across the Buffalo River to the Erbie Campground.)

From the parking lot the trail takes off STRAIGHT out into the woods (be sure that you get on the correct trail, which is on the left—a "volunteer" trail or two leave the parking area too, but don't go anyplace). It works its way down a hill and across a small stream, then eases its way up the other side, passing beneath a power line. There is one spot where the trail goes next to what I call an "N" tree—a tree that in its early years probably had another tree fall on it and bend it over, then it continued to grow up, forming an "N" shape in its trunk.

The hillside gets kind of rocky, and there are some nice large trees scattered about. The trail continues up the hillside gradually, then levels off, then rises up just a little, up and across a flat-topped ridge. It begins to head down the hillside through a thick stand of trees, several of them nice large pines, then goes through an area with lots of rock outcrops. In this area you'll be able to look out and see the emerging drainage area in front of you. Soon you come out on top of the edge of a tall bluff at .8 mile, and have some great views into and across this hollow—Hideout Hollow, and off to the right into the Cecil Creek Valley. This spot, from this point on up the drainage, is spectacular.

The trail turns to the left here, and continues along on top of the bluff. *A word of caution—there are lots of tall bluffs in this area, and if you have little ones with you, please keep a hold on them at all times.* There are plenty of foot paths away from the bluff so use those when you need to. There are a couple of signs of past man in here—a small rock structure and a couple of old car doors. The trail runs back away from the bluff a little, and you can begin to hear water, a sign that neater stuff is ahead!

The trail passes through a cedar grove, where there isn't much of a definite trail tread—just follow along the best you can.

The trail goes downhill just a little ways to a creek. This is the head of Hideout Hollow, and down below the trail is the large waterfall that we've been hearing. There are also some other lesser falls both below the trail and a couple of hundred feet upstream too. It's rather thick across the way, but you can work your way around to get a better view of the big falls, and the bluffline that you've been walking on. Looks like a great place to "hide out" don't you think? The end of the trail is right at 1.0 mile from the parking lot.

To return to the trailhead simply go back out the same way that you came in, making it a nice two-mile hike.

If you need to go #2 in the woods and don't have a shovel to dig a hole but you do have toilet paper, put your "stuff" under a rock so other people don't have to see it.

The turkey is a fast runner and can out run a fox. Turkeys can also swim.

Triple Falls (aka Twin Falls)
.5 mile round trip

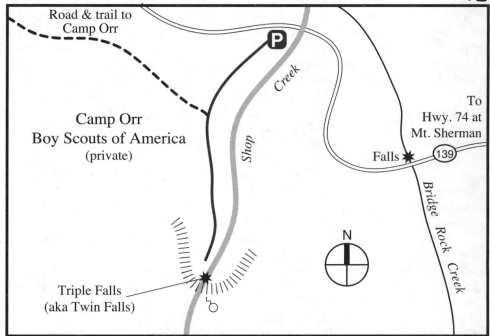

Road & trail to Camp Orr

Camp Orr
Boy Scouts of America
(private)

Creek

Shop

To
Hwy. 74 at
Mt. Sherman

Falls ✳ (139)

Bridge Rock Creek

N

Triple Falls
(aka Twin Falls)

Triple Falls (aka Twin Falls at Camp Orr). This is one of the most scenic easy waterfalls to get to—the WHOLE family can walk right up to the edge of the creek near the base for a perfect view. It has long been called Twin Falls, but we call it Triple Falls for two reasons: first, when the falls are running well there are always three falls, not two. And secondly we have so many other waterfalls named Twin Falls in Arkansas it is simply less confusing to call this one something else. The name "twin" comes from the fact (we think) that there are actually two water sources that feed the falls from above—one is the creek (the right falls), and the other is a spring up to the left that feeds the two falls on the left. So now you know. *No dogs are allowed on the trail.*

The turnoff to get to the parking area is located between Jasper and Low Gap. From Jasper, go west on Hwy. 74 to Mt. Sherman and turn right at the sign for Kyles Landing (OR go east from Low Gap on Hwy. 74 for 5.2 miles to Mt. Sherman and turn left at the Kyles Landing Sign). The road is gravel and normally not marked with a road number. Go 1.0 mile and bear right at the fork—the left fork goes down into Kyles Landing. Continue heading down the hill for another 1.8 miles until you hit bottom, right after crossing a creek, and park at the edge of a field (there may be a sign for Twin Falls there). NOTE that the last mile of this road is *really steep* and muddy!

From the parking area head to the left on a trail that follows that creek you just crossed upstream into the woods—it's a level hike of less than .25 mile. There will be another trail that comes in from your right, but just keep going STRAIGHT AHEAD and you will come right to the falls.

NOTE that the land beyond the parking area is the Boy Scout facility Camp Orr, and generally off limits to the public.

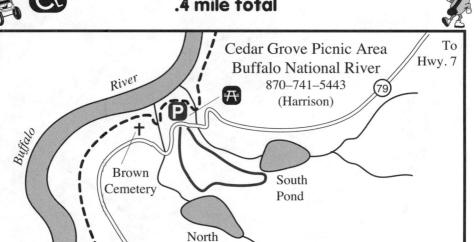

Cedar Grove Picnic Area
Buffalo National River
870–741–5443
(Harrison)

To
Hwy. 7

79

River

Buffalo

P

+

Brown
Cemetery

South
Pond

North
Pond

Buffalo River Trail

To
Erbie

N

Ponds Loop. There is a small picnic area that is located two miles down the gravel road to Erbie Campground (the turnoff is on Hwy. 7 between Jasper and Pruitt), that is called Cedar Grove Picnic Area. There is a nice overlook of the Buffalo River there, and it is a terrific spot for a picnic lunch. Also the Buffalo River Trail comes right through the far end of the picnic area. And there are a couple of short trails that lead off to two ponds—South Pond and North Pond. *No dogs are allowed on the trail.*

The parking lot is on the River side of the road, which is where the picnic tables and the overlook are located. The two trails take off across the road from the parking lot. The trail to the left (South Pond) is made of hard-packed gravel, and is accessible via wheelchair and stroller. This little trail runs nearly level for .1 mile out to the pond, where you will find a neat observation deck that goes out over the edge of the water.

The trail from that point on is a regular narrow trail, and not wheelchair nor stroller accessible. From the observation deck the trail heads up into the woods, easing up the wooded hillside just a little bit, then comes back down again to the edge of the North Pond. TURN RIGHT at the corner of the pond and you will loop on back to the parking area making a total hike of about .4 mile. These are nice, clear little ponds, and a stroll to visit them is just the ticket to help work off that picnic lunch!

Don't eat wild mushrooms.

Mill Creek Loop
2.2 miles round trip

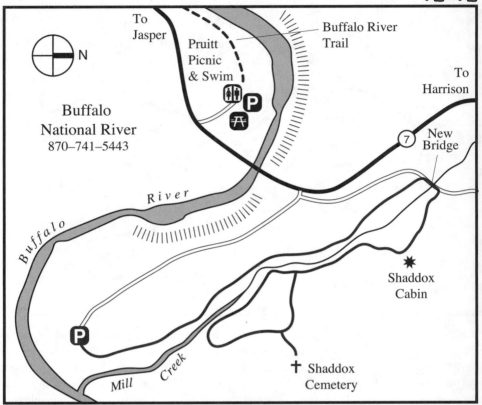

To Jasper

Buffalo River Trail

Pruitt Picnic & Swim

To Harrison

Buffalo National River
870–741–5443

N

7 New Bridge

River

Buffalo

Shaddox Cabin

P

Mill Creek

✝ Shaddox Cemetery

Mill Creek Loop. If you are traveling down National Scenic 7 Byway between Harrison and Jasper, you should stop at Pruitt and hike this short trail. It is located at Buffalo National River, just off of Hwy. 7 at the lower end of the Pruitt Access. It is easy to walk, and goes through a variety of forest and stream environments, not to mention a couple of historical spots. *Dogs are allowed on this trail, with a 6' leash.*

The trailhead is on the north side of the river (turn right at the "Pruitt Access" sign). Go down to the access area and find the trailhead sign—park off to the left.

The trail takes off level from the trailhead beside the Buffalo River. This is a nice, easy, level walk for the most part. It swings to the left and begins to follow Mill Creek, a quiet medium-sized creek. The trail runs through a pretty open bottomland hardwood forest. It veers to the right and rises up over a small bluff.

The trail continues alongside the creek until it comes to a dirt road—TURN RIGHT on the road and cross Mill Creek on a low cement bridge. Just across the other side, TURN RIGHT off of the road onto the trail again—there is a sign. *A new county road bridge was built high above in 2020 just downstream of the low cement bridge.*

This section works its way downstream and gradually uphill, and heads up to the Shaddox Cabin. This structure has actually been recycled. It was built using the logs from an old log home which stood near this site. Re–use of old buildings was characteristic of thrifty Ozark pioneers. The trail crosses in front of the cabin, and then works its way back down the small

40

hill again. It swings through the forest and comes to a trail intersection—go STRAIGHT and you'll end up back at the creek crossing. TURN LEFT for the continuation of the trail.

The trail goes through an old grown–up field, and under a power line, then back into the woods, and to another trail intersection. TURN LEFT, and a short spur leads up the hill to Shaddox Cemetery. This one is larger than most you'll see in the area. Ezekiel Shaddox, the builder of the original log house, is buried in this cemetery. When you are finished looking around, head back down to the trail intersection and continue STRAIGHT ahead.

This section gradually comes down off the hill, through the woods and back to Mill Creek. It TURNS RIGHT and heads back upstream alongside the creek—follow the trail back to the cement bridge and back to the trailhead.

Have your parents pack some duck tape. If you get into seed ticks, duck tape pulls them off real well. Duck tape also takes out splinters, and it doesn't even hurt.

Fish sleep with their eyes open because they have no eyelids.

Koen Interpretive Loop
.5 mile total

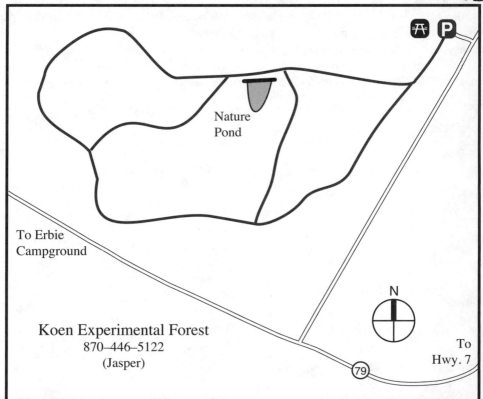

Nature Pond

To Erbie
Campground

Koen Experimental Forest
870–446–5122
(Jasper)

N

To
Hwy. 7

79

Koen Interpretive Loop. If you are looking for a nice leisurely stroll through a variety of tree species, this is the trail for you. This trail is GREAT for the really young kids and perfect for a first outing into the woods. There are at least 34 different kinds of trees and other plants identified along this short loop. To get to the trailhead, turn off of Hwy. 7 about 2.3 miles south of Pruitt at the Erbie Campground sign, go less than a half mile and turn right. After a couple of hundred yards, turn left into the trailhead parking area. There are several picnic tables here, and also benches scattered along the trail.

The Henry R. Koen Experimental Forest was established in 1950 to develop scientific principles of forest management and to define and evaluate land management concerns. There is a great deal of research that has been and is going on in this small tract of land. Mr. Koen was Supervisor of the Ozark National Forest from 1922—1939.

There really isn't much of a description that I can give you here—you just need to get out and walk this one. Be sure to pick up a trail guide that is available at the trailhead—it describes all of the plant species that are highlighted. These include: black cherry, winged elm, prickly pear, red mulberry, plume grass, common persimmon, box elder, winged sumac, wild plum, honey locust, sycamore, white ash, mockernut hickory, shortleaf pine, pitch pine, eastern redbud, black locust, black raspberry, buckbrush, Indian cherry, black walnut, eastern white pine, Virginia pine, sassafras, tulip poplar, loblolly pine, eastern red cedar, flowering dogwood, hackberry, chinkapin oak, summer grape, chokevine, blackberry and southern red oak. There aren't any bluffs or dangerous areas for the kids and the trail is level, so enjoy.

Alum Cove Loop
1.1 miles total

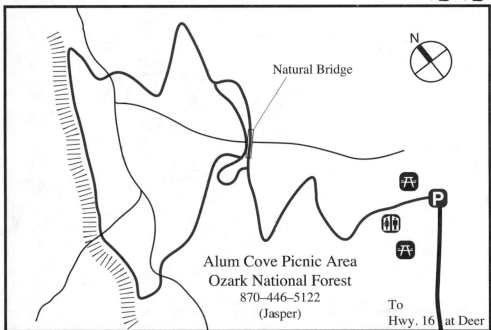

Natural Bridge

N

Alum Cove Picnic Area
Ozark National Forest
870–446–5122
(Jasper)

To
Hwy. 16 at Deer

Alum Cove Loop. This wonderful little trail visits one of the largest natural rock bridges in this part of the country. It loops around past a nice bluffline too. There is tall timber, and lots of wildflowers, including a rare variety of Shooting Star. No camping is allowed, but it's a great spot for a picnic.

To get to Alum Cove, take Hwy. 7 south out of Jasper. Turn right on Hwy. 16 towards the community of Deer. After about a mile turn right off of Hwy. 16 onto Forest Road #1206 (paved). Take the forest road to the picnic area sign and turn right.

From the parking area the trail goes through the picnic area and heads on down the hill, then switchbacks down until it reaches the natural bridge—an *awesome* spot (there are several benches along the way). You can walk right out on top of the bridge—it's 130 feet long and 12 feet thick. During the wet season there is a waterfall or two that pours into the open area behind it. The trail loops on down underneath the bridge too—a most impressive sight!

From the base of the bridge the trail continues on down the hill a little and crosses a stream, then works its way up the other side to a wonderful bluffline. The first thing that you see along the bluff is a cave entrance. It doesn't go in very far, but it does have two different entrances and is a neat little spot. The kids love this area and can spend hours here. Relax, have a snack and let them explore.

The trail TURNS RIGHT at the bluff and follows it along for a while. The bluff (and natural bridge) are made from sandstone, and so has been easily carved out by eons of wind and water. At one point the bluff splits and you can walk behind it. In many spots the bluff is covered with lots of lichens, mosses and ferns. During the wet season, there is a nice water-fall that pours over the bluff. All too soon the trail leaves the bluff, drops back down to and across the small stream, and heads back up to the other end of the natural bridge. Follow the trail back up to the trailhead—take it slow and easy.

Round Top Mountain Loop
2.3 to 3.6 miles total

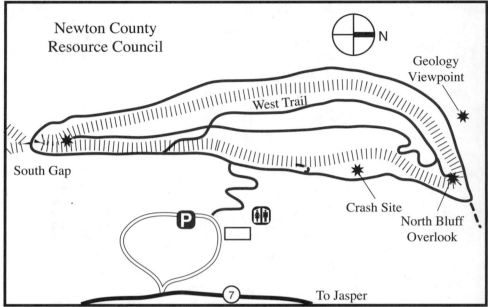

Newton County
Resource Council

N

Geology
Viewpoint

West Trail

South Gap

Crash Site

North Bluff
Overlook

P

To Jasper

7

Round Top Mountain Loop. No doubt this is one of the most scenic trails in Arkansas, and also there is some rare history to go with it—the remains of a bomber that crashed in 1948. The first part of the trail is all uphill, but it soon levels out and visits a terrific bluffline with great views, and has tons of wildflower beds all over the place. To get to the trailhead, take Hwy. 7 south out of Jasper a couple of miles and turn right at the sign, then park at the small building. One of the engines from the bomber had been on display at the trailhead, but it was stolen. Everything is owned and maintained by the Newton County Resource Council.

If you hike all of the trail that is described here, it will total 3.6 miles. You can shorten that by more than a mile (2.3 miles total hike) by remaining down below the bluff and not going up on top at the 1.7 mile intersection—you'll still have one of the very best hikes in the state! Most of the trail is very easy to hike, but the initial climb up to the base of the bluff will really take it out of ya. If you survive that climb, the rest is easy.

The trail starts out by climbing the steep hillside in four winding switchbacks— there are benches at every switchback! In fact, there are more than 30 benches located all along the route. At .2 mile there is a trail intersection—TURN RIGHT to visit the entire trail. It is all level now as the trail goes along a flat bench that is located just below the massive sandstone bluff that is up to your left. Not only is the bluff beautiful, but you'll find thousands of wildflowers here in spring and early summer. At .4 mile there is a small trail that goes to the left up to the base of the bluff, and to a little tunnel cave. The main trail continues along the bench and comes to the crash site at .5 mile. There is an old rock wall and a bronze plaque that lists the date and names of the crew. You may find bits and pieces of the B–25 bomber that smashed into the hillside—like the wildflowers, these are all protected—*please* do not remove anything. Remain quiet at this site, and remember the sacrifice that our military folks make in order for us to live free in this country.

The trail continues along near the base of the bluff, past another little trail that drops down the hill to the right to a lookout point—if you are going to the top, the view is much better from up there. The main trail curves around the nose of the bluffline to the left, and comes to the Geology Viewpoint at .7 mile, a special area with giant moss-covered blocks of sandstone and a terrific view.

The trail remains level as it curves around to the left and to the back side of the mountain, past the 1.0 mile point. There are some views out towards the Little Buffalo River Valley, and scores of wildflower fields on the forest floor. By 1.5 miles the trail has bumped up to a break in the bluffline known as South Gap, another special spot! Once through the gap the trail turns to the left and remains close to the base of the bluff, going past a Native American campsite area, and through a split in the bluffline, all of it is spectacular.

There is a trail intersection at 1.7 miles—TURN LEFT and go up a flight of stairs that will lead you to the top of the mountain. There is another intersection ahead—TURN RIGHT to head up to the main overlook (you will return to this spot via the West Trail). The trail eases up the hill some, following the top of the ridge, past milepoint 2.0, then tops out at the high point on the mountain. From there the trail begins to ease on down the hill to the right, and drops on down to another intersection—TURN RIGHT, then follow the trail on down to where it ends at the North Bluff Overlook at 2.3 miles, a terrific area with a 200 degree view!

Now, take the trail back up to the last intersection and GO STRAIGHT, which will take you around the back side of the mountain on the West Trail. It is level and there are some great views. It will intersect with the main trail at 2.9 miles—TURN RIGHT and take the short spur out to the top of South Gap, another great view, then return to the same intersection and TURN RIGHT and go back down the long flight of steps. TURN LEFT at the bottom of the steps, which will take you back to the last intersection at 3.4 miles—TURN RIGHT and follow the switchbacks to the trailhead, a total hike of 3.6 miles. You can shorten this hike by selecting only parts of the trail. The overlooks on the top loop on Round Top Mountain are protected by railings but watch your kids just in case.

When you are hiking have a taller person go in front of you. They will get all of the cobwebs down.

White on a mother bobcat's ears and tail helps her babies keep her in sight as they follow her.

Collier Homestead Trail
.9 mile round trip

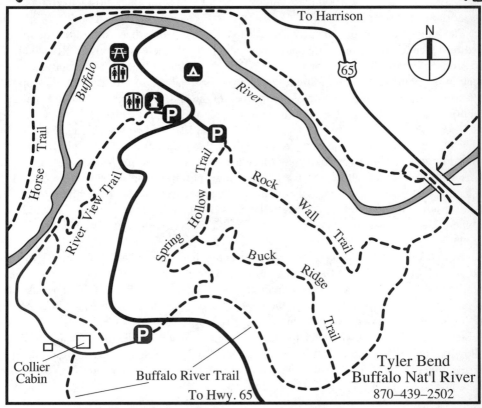

To Harrison

N

65

Buffalo

River

Horse Trail

River View Trail

Spring Hollow Trail

Rock Wall Trail

Buck Ridge Trail

P

P

P

Collier Cabin

Buffalo River Trail

To Hwy. 65

Tyler Bend
Buffalo Nat'l River
870–439–2502

Collier Homestead/River View Trail. Talk about an incredible view! This trail does lead you to the top of a very tall bluff, however there is an overlook there with a railing, so I feel pretty comfortable having kids there. Still, keep an eye on them. There are plenty of trails at Tyler Bend to hike, but to us, this is the best. We will take you in and out the same direction even though the trail can be turned into a loop trail. The loop goes pretty close to the edge and has no railing on down so we chose not to go there. *No dogs are allowed on the trail*.

Tyler Bend is one of the main visitor facilities on the Buffalo River. There is a nice Visitor Center and museum there, as well as campgrounds, picnic areas, and canoe access. Tyler Bend is located off of Hwy. 65 between St. Joe and Marshall, just south of the Hwy. 65 bridge across the Buffalo. Once you pull into the park it is 1.2 miles to the Collier Homestead parking area located on your left.

The very first part of this hike is actually the Collier Homestead Trail, then once you pass the homestead it becomes the River View Trail—you will follow the River View Trail out to the overlook, then turn around and come back.

You will begin heading to the right of the big sign toward the Collier Homestead. This is a wide, level path and a jogger stroller will probably make this trail just fine. At a little less than .1 mile there is a trail that takes off to your right (this is the return loop if you choose to come back that way), continue STRAIGHT ahead. At the far end of the homestead at the end of the fence the trail curves to the right and heads STRAIGHT ahead, staying level. There is

46

a trail at the homestead that takes off to the left (this is the Buffalo River Trail that goes far upstream and connects with the Ozark Highlands Trail), but you want to continue STRAIGHT ahead toward the next old building (this now becomes the River View Trail). At just over .4 mile you will come to the stunning overlook. Good thing you brought your camera!

At this point you have several choices. Either turn around and head back to the parking area the same way that you came in (.9 mile total hike); or continue on down the River View Trail along the bluffline (can be dangerous for kids!) and then either loop back to the parking area (total hike of just over one mile), or go all the way down to the Visitor Center, which is far below (a total hike of 1.3 miles). If you choose to hike all the way down, you can connect with one of the three other trails that begin near the Visitor Center and hike back up the hill, making a complete loop of up to 4.0 miles and turning it into a three hotdogger trail.

Scavenger Hunt ? **What was the father's name at the Collier Homestead?**

 Toads don't give you warts. Stress does.

Cirrus Clouds look like a horse's tail. If you see these it means fair-weather and a great day for hiking.

Indian Rockhouse Loop
3.0 miles total

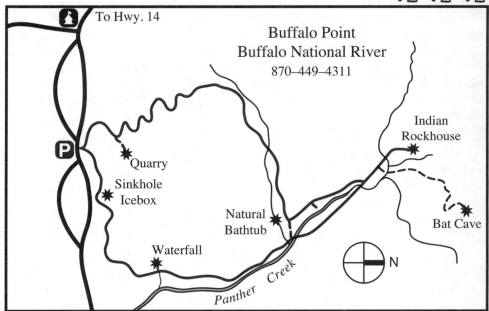

Indian Rockhouse Loop. Buffalo Point is the most developed area within Buffalo National River. Besides a Visitor Center, there are several campgrounds, cabins, a restaurant, picnic areas, river access, and a number of hiking trails. Most of these trails just connect facilities, but one, the Indian Rockhouse Trail, is a wonderful three–mile loop into a scenic area, and visits one of the largest bluff overhangs in the Ozarks. *No dogs are allowed on the trail.*

Buffalo Point is located off of Hwy. 14, between the turnoff to Rush, and the Hwy. 14 bridge over the Buffalo River. Follow the signs—the road is all paved. The main trailhead parking area is located just past the Visitor Center. You can pick up a trail booklet there that is keyed to identification signs along the trail. (Note—we've heard the signs have not been maintained by the park service so you may not find them.)

The trail begins across the road from the trailhead, and heads down an old road. The return trail comes in from the left just as you start down the hill. Near the bottom of the hill, the trail turns to the right and follows beside a small creek. The first sign that you come to is "Poison Ivy." That is fitting, since a lot of you that hike this will get poison ivy—so be careful—there is a lot of the stuff out here in the woods! (See page 143 for a drawing of the plant.) The next sign is "Ferns and Mayapples." You should come in late April and May to see these. The trail continues on, and passes a small bluff to the right. "Smooth Sumac" is next, and in late September and early October this stuff turns a wonderful color. Just beyond, the trail leaves the old road bed that it has been following and is plain trail now.

Next is the "Sinkhole Icebox" on the left. A nice spot to be in the heat of summer! Be careful not to slip in. The trail continues on fairly level, out through and past our next sign "Hardwood Forest." Then the trail begins to drop off down the hill just a little, past the "Cedar Glade" sign. Just after, be sure to TURN LEFT down the hill on a slab rock. And the trail keeps going down for a little while, and swings around to the left.

Then you encounter another beautiful spot, a wonderful waterfall. The trail actually crosses under it, then swings back to the right. The bluff that forms the waterfall is pretty neat too, and the trail follows it to the "Bluff Mammals" sign.

The trail heads on down the hill, past the bluff, and comes alongside the small creek that formed the waterfall. Then you pass "Abandoned Mine," and you can see the remains of a small zinc mine. Down to Panther Creek you go, as the trail turns to the left and begins to follow the creek upstream. This is a nice little creek—you'll see a lot of it.

There are lots of bluffs around, on both sides of the creek, as you pass the "Moist Bluff" sign. But the real treasure in this area is the creek. This is probably one of the best streamside walks in the state. But not for long, as the trail soon eases up the hill to "Small Cave." It's a neat little cave, with a sinkhole coming into the ceiling at one point.

Just past this cave you come out onto an old paved road—TURN RIGHT on this road, and you will come to an intersection. The main trail continues STRAIGHT AHEAD on the road, but if you are getting tuckered out, you can TURN LEFT for a short cut to the return loop.

The main trail crosses Panther Creek, and heads up a hill (still on the old road), then levels off and looks down onto the creek. You will pass Pebble Spring, which you'll visit on the return loop. Just beyond, you'll cross a rock slab, which is nice during the wet season. Then the trail passes by the "Calamint" sign, and another trail intersection (it's another short cut over to the return trail)—stay STRAIGHT AHEAD to get to the Indian Rockhouse.

At the "Sculptured Bedrock" sign you'll encounter another great spot which is worth a closer look. Just past this area, the trail crosses Panther Creek. The "real" return loop takes off to the left here—continue on STRAIGHT AHEAD for the main trail (still on the old road). It will head up another short but steep hill, then drop down again, to a trail intersection.

The main trail goes STRAIGHT AHEAD at the trail intersection, crosses Panther Creek, and heads right up to the Indian Rockhouse. This is a marvelous place. There is a large sinkhole in the roof to the right, a creek running through the back of the overhang, and just lots of neat stuff for you to explore. There are even some genuine cave formations here—the "stalactites" point down from the ceiling, "stalagmites" are growing up from the floor, and there are "curtains" and "flowstone" along the wall.

After a good rest, you're ready to head back to the trailhead. Begin by going back the same way that you came, across the creek and past the trail to Bat Cave. Just before you cross Panther Creek again, TURN RIGHT at the intersection, and follow the trail upstream. It crosses a bridge, and comes to the Sculptured Rock area that you saw from the other side. Then it meets up with a short spur trail that drops down to Pebble Spring. The main trail swings to the right, up a small hill and then levels off. After a little ways you come to another wonderful sculptured rock area on the creek—this area wasn't seen on the trip in from the other side, and I would definitely rate it as spectacular! A cool spot to spend some time.

Just beyond is a trail intersection. Back to the left is the way that you came in. TURN RIGHT at this intersection to continue with the main trail out. This is the "Natural Bathtub" . The trail follows this small stream up the drainage through a cedar glade. It crosses the stream at a pretty little spot, heads up the hill a little, swings back to the right and levels off.

It continues up the drainage, with the little stream down off on the right, past the "Watershed" sign. Here it gets more serious about climbing up the hill, and in fact does just that—CLIMBS. Up several switchbacks it goes, to an intersection. The left fork goes over to the old "Fossil Quarry," a short walk. The main trail TURNS RIGHT and continues up the hill on an old roadbed past the "Dogwood" sign.

As the trail tops out, you pass through a wooden gate, cross an old road with another wooden gate off to the left, and continue into the woods on level trail (you are now alongside the paved road that you are parked on). You will shortly come out at the trailhead where you started. What a great hike!

The next seven trails are all located near the dam of Bull Shoals Lake in three different parks—Bull Shoals State Park, Lakeview Park, and Gaston's Resort (this one is private, but their two wonderful trails are open to the public). You can spend an entire weekend exploring these trails that are all close to one another. Bull Shoals Dam is located on Hwy. 178 northwest of Mountain Home between the communities of Lakeview and Bull Shoals.

Lakeside Loop
1.0 mile total

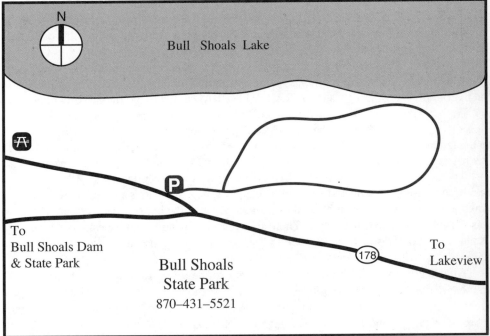

Lakeside Loop. This little trail is actually part of Bull Shoals State Park, although it is located up at the dam level and not down below the dam like the rest of the park and the other trails. To get to the trailhead go towards Lakeview from the dam and take a sharp turn to the left. Do not turn right into Bull Shoals State Park. As you turn to the left you will see a pavilion up on a hill on your left. Turn left and head toward the playground, restrooms and picnic area. When you reach the top of the hill, turn right. The Lakeside Trailhead parking is at the end of this road on your left.

The trail takes off behind some picnic tables and a fire grate. It heads down some gravel steps towards the lake. After about 100 feet once you enter the woods you will come to an intersection. Head to the left. This is a beautiful view, especially when the leaves are off. The trail will remain fairly level as it follows along side the lake. Look back to your left and you will be able to see the dam. At about .4 mile you will come to an overlook. GREAT place to have a snack. Continue along the ridge on the level, walking upstream from the dam. The trail curves to the right and heads up a slight hill. It curves to the right again and remains level all the way back to the trailhead.

This is a beautiful little trail that is great for beginners!

Dogwood Nature Trail
3.0 miles round trip

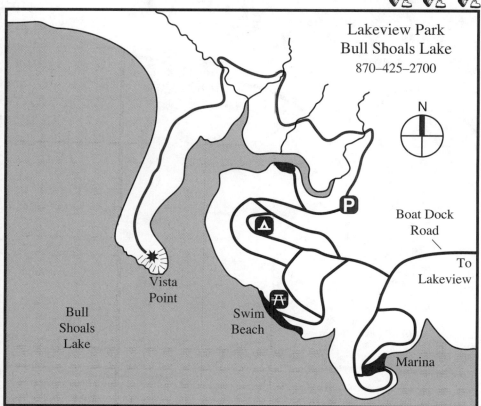

Lakeview Park
Bull Shoals Lake
870–425–2700

N

P

Boat Dock
Road

To
Lakeview

Vista
Point

Bull
Shoals
Lake

Swim
Beach

Marina

Dogwood Nature Trail. This trail winds through the woods just above Bull Shoals Lake, and ends at a spectacular set of bluffs that disappear deep into the waters. The Bluebird population is extremely high all along this trail. It is located at Lakeview Park, just outside the community of Lakeview, east of Bull Shoals Dam.

The trailhead is located at the back of the park in camping area C off of Boat Dock Road (keep turning right). If it is during the winter area C may be closed so your hike may be a little longer. The trail heads down a flight of steps, quickly levels off behind several houses, then eases up the hill. It drops down the hill as it swings back to the left, then crosses the first of several small streams. It heads back uphill a little, swings around the hillside as it levels off, then drops back down into another small ravine. It does this four times. There are numerous trees that have name tags telling what they are—some interesting ones! Mile 1.0 is just beyond the one marked "Eastern Red Cedar." And just beyond that at 1.1 mile, there is a trail intersection, and a spectacular view of the lake! TURN LEFT here and head down the narrow ridgetop (be sure to watch for this turn on the way back). The views on both sides are great, and the trail passes through a nice cedar glade.

The trail drops down the hill some to the low spot in the ridge, just above the lake—you can see the dam to the left. It heads back up the hill, levels off, and comes to the end of the trail at 1.5 miles. This is a terrific spot, and worth every step to get here, with craggy bluffs and a wonderful view. Return to the trailhead the same way that you came (unless you want to swim!), and remember to make the right-hand turn back at the other end of the ridge.

Big Bluff Loop
1.8 miles total

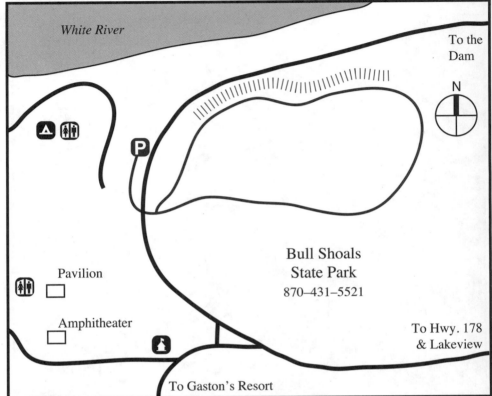

White River

To the
Dam

N

P

Pavilion

Amphitheater

Bull Shoals
State Park
870–431–5521

To Hwy. 178
& Lakeview

To Gaston's Resort

Big Bluff Loop. The Big Bluff Trail is a loop trail that does pass through an area that is high on a bluff. This bluff is not fenced off or is in any other way protected. Please watch your children carefully. This trail is not recommended for the very young.

To get to the trailhead from the dam, head east and turn right towards the State Park. As you enter the park turn to the right towards the dam instead of going towards the Visitor Center. Go about .5 mile and the trailhead is an open space on the left with plenty of parking. There is a big, make that HUGE, sign there for the Big Bluff Trail. The trail takes off to the left of the parking area and begins on level ground, actually you will be hiking on the remains of an old railroad bed. The trail is blazed with yellow blazes.

The trail curves back to the left and heads toward the highway. Once you reach the highway, PARENTS: WATCH YOUR KIDS—there is a lot of traffic on this road. Head directly across the highway and into the trees. After a couple of hundred yards you will come to an intersection with an information sign (may not be any information on it). We will head toward the right, however this is a loop trail so it can be hiked in either direction.

The trail is very rocky (with plenty of moss along the way), so watch your footing. The first half of this trail seems to mainly be going in the up direction. Take your time and enjoy the moss covered rocks. The trail begins to curve to the left and will head down a slope. The next ridge is just up ahead and you can see that there is a "view" coming. The first sight that you may see are houses, however, be sure to look down, the White River is down below. Once on top of this ridge it is level walking. There are a ton of birds along this trail. However, the river may be hard to see when the leaves are on the trees. You will start to head down a slope and move closer to the bluffline, be sure to watch the kids in this area, and KEEP THEM ON THE TRAIL. You will come to an overlook with a bench. A beautiful place to stop and have a snack, rest and watch the river roll by. Keep away from the edge of the bluff though, it is quite a dropoff with a highway down below.

The trail continues along the bluff for 50 feet and then curves back to the left and away from the bluff. You will enjoy a gentle slope back to the intersection that began your hike.

Memorial Wildflower Loop
.8 mile total

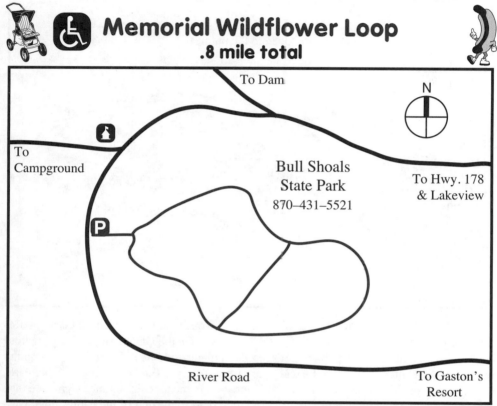

Memorial Wildflower Loop. This is a short, paved trail leading through a meadow that is filled with wildflowers and plenty of wildlife activity in the springtime. From the dam, turn right into the State Park and turn left heading in the direction of the Visitor Center, then follow as the road curves sharply to the left to the trailhead.

You'll begin the trail heading to the right. This trail is paved, fairly level and is great for strollers and/or wheelchairs. There are benches along the way to sit and enjoy the flowers and wildlife. The trail meanders through a meadow and is a loop trail leading you back to the parking area. In the center of the loop you will find a nice pavilion area with benches. The trailhead area can be seen at all times from the trail so there is no need to worry about getting lost. Relax and enjoy the trail!

Bluebird Trail. Stop at the Visitor Center and pick up a map that shows bluebird houses throughout the park—these make up the Bluebird Trail. This trail can be turned into a delight-ful scavenger hunt. Have the kids look at the map, and then find the bluebird houses. It is a GREAT learning experience about reading maps. There is plenty of bluebird activity in this park during the spring and summer months. All are bluebirds of happiness!

Scavenger Hunt ? **How many bluebird houses are there on the Bluebird Trail?**

White River Nature Loop
1.5 miles total

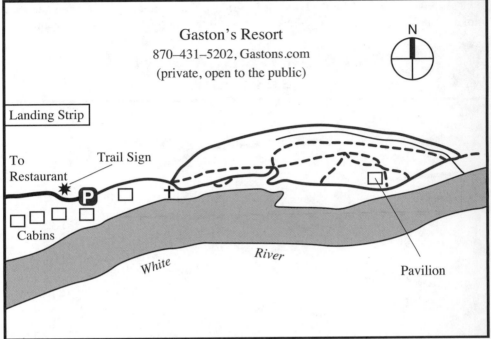

Gaston's Resort
870–431–5202, Gastons.com
(private, open to the public)

N

Landing Strip

To Restaurant

Trail Sign

P

Cabins

White   River

Pavilion

White River Nature Loop. There are a couple of wonderful nature trails at Gaston's Resort, one of the best and most famous trout fishing resorts in the United States. They are kind enough to open them to the public, and keep them maintained well. Be sure to stop by the restaurant there after your hike for a real Ozark treat! To get to Gaston's from the State Park, continue past the Memorial Wildflower Trail until you come to their entrance sign, then turn right. When you come to the restaurant, turn left and go to the end of the cabins, then park just beyond the "White River Nature Trail" sign at Cabin #77.

The trail begins between two wooden fence posts down what looks like a gravel driveway. There are huge cottonwood trees here. You will pass by another cabin and continue STRAIGHT ahead. There are many loops through here with plenty of wildflowers to see along the way. We will take the outside loop but feel free to explore all you want. There are benches along the trail, plenty of wildlife and tons of bluebird houses. At .1 mile the trail curves to the right. There are interpretive signs along your hike and you will be walking on level ground along the White River. Continue along staying close to the river. The trail curves back to the left and comes to a 5 trail intersection. Turn back to your right and stay close to the river. Pass the pavilion at .6 mile and continue STRAIGHT ahead. The trail curves to the left at .7 mile and comes out into an open field, TURN LEFT. Follow this trail all the way back to the original intersection. At the original intersection TURN RIGHT to head back to the parking area.

Treat all animals with respect.

Ozark Nature Loop
.9 mile total

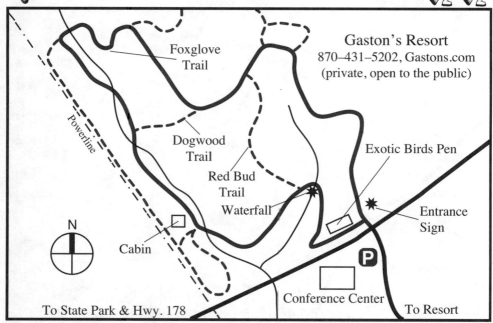

Foxglove Trail

Gaston's Resort
870–431–5202, Gastons.com
(private, open to the public)

Powerline

Dogwood Trail

Red Bud Trail

Exotic Birds Pen

Waterfall

N

Cabin

Entrance Sign

P

Conference Center

To State Park & Hwy. 178

To Resort

Ozark Nature Loop. This is the second trail at Gaston's, and is actually many trails in one. When you come into the Gaston's Resort area you will see bird pens on your left—turn right and then turn right again and park at the Conference Lodge. The trail begins between the bird pens and the sign with the waterfall.

This is a wonderful hike in the spring with the dogwood trees in bloom and all of the wildflowers. There are plenty of loops to explore but, you will be following along the Dogwood and Foxglove Trails. Bikes are allowed on these trails. After the trail leaves the bird pen area it curves to the left and heads uphill, then curves to the right and continues uphill. There are amazing old antiques and plenty of things to look at along the way. At .2 mile you will come to an intersection with the Lost Jeep Loop, TURN LEFT and follow the Dogwood Trail sign. At the next intersection TURN LEFT, notice the odd benches. Shortly after you will come to another intersection and if you need to head back to the trailhead, now is your chance, TURN LEFT...otherwise, to continue the hike TURN RIGHT. At the next intersection TURN RIGHT and you will now be on the Foxglove Trail. At .4 mile another intersection appears and you will TURN LEFT and head downhill. At the next intersection TURN LEFT, this will be at .5 mile. Through here you will be walking by a little stream that if it is running will be just delightful. At .6 mile you will intersect with the Dogwood Trail, continue STRAIGHT ahead. Shortly after you will curve around and see a neat little cabin with an old tractor out in front.....Do you think there are any cowboys in there? Right after the cabin you will come to an intersection, TURN LEFT and head downhill, follow this back to the trailhead. At .8 mile you will have another creek crossing and when the water is running there will be a waterfall on your right. The trail curves around and ends up in front of the bird pens. There are benches in front of the pens so you can rest and watch these amazing birds at play.

Scavenger Hunt ? What is the name of the old tractor in front of the cabin?

Big Trees Loop
.9 mile total

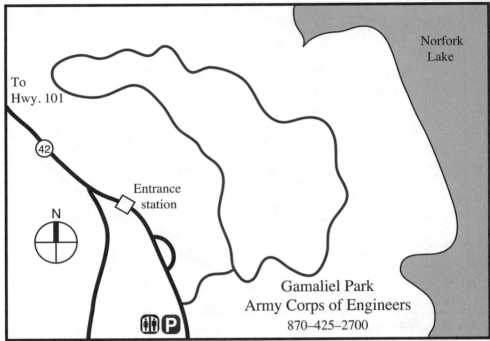

To Hwy. 101

42

N

Entrance station

Norfork Lake

Gamaliel Park
Army Corps of Engineers
870–425–2700

Big Trees Loop. Here is a neat trail that was built by a single volunteer, and it winds through some very large pine trees along the banks of Norfork Lake. To get to the trailhead in the Gamaliel Recreation Area from Mountain Home take Hwy. 62 east to Hwy. 101 and go north. Go seven miles to CR#42/Fout Rd. and turn right. Go through the park entrance and park at the next restrooms directly on your right. The trail begins across the road and to your left a little bit. Look for the blazes.

The trail heads downhill and comes to an intersection at a little less than .1 mile, TURN LEFT. There are some beautiful, huge trees through here. The trail meanders back and forth with a little bit of up and downing and there are some rocky places through here. At .4 mile the trail curves back to the right and heads downhill somewhat, there will be some great views of the lake during leaf-off. At a little over .4 mile there is a huge oak tree that suffered a major lightning strike which you can see on both sides of the tree. At .8 mile the trail drops down into a little drainage and heads back up the other side, curve to the right and head back uphill. The trail turns sharply back to the left at .9 mile and continues its trek up. Shortly after you will arrive back at the original intersection. Turn left to head back to the parking area.

If you hike after it rains pull back branches of trees and flick them, you'll get the person behind you wet.

56

Salem City Park
.6 mile total

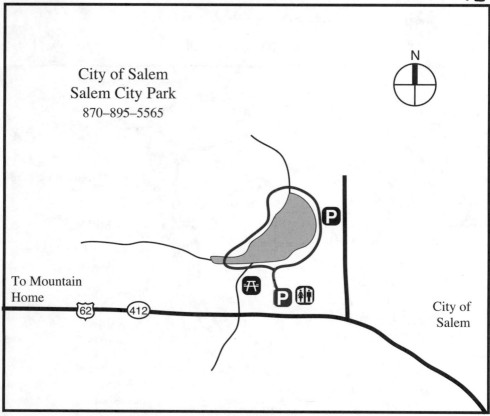

City of Salem
Salem City Park
870–895–5565

N

To Mountain
Home

62 412

City of
Salem

Salem City Park. Located on the north side of Hwy. 62 the Salem City Park is a great little place to get out, stretch your legs, use the restroom and have a picnic lunch. From the intersection of Hwy. 62 and Hwy. 412 in Mountain Home, head 31. 5 miles east. This paved trail circles around a lake with great fishing (per the locals), plenty of ducks to watch and a playground to work off some energy. As you circle the lake you will see a pier that juts out into the lake giving you great fishing access. There are benches scattered along the way for resting and relaxing with a very peaceful view of the water. If you start out to the right you will head down a steep hill on the far side of the lake, if you start out to the left you will climb this steep section.

Blanchard Springs Trail
.3 mile round trip

Mirror Lake Loop
1.3 miles total

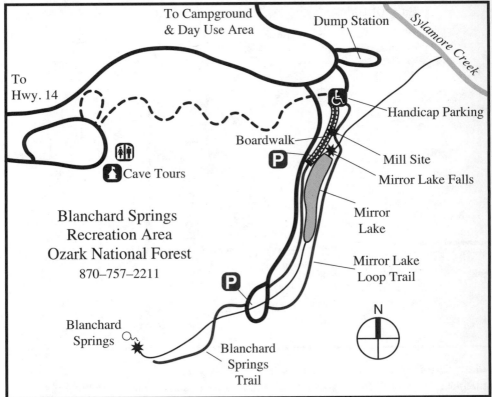

Blanchard Springs Trail. Blanchard Springs is a magical place that has attracted visitors for many generations. Plus, the spring and falls run all summer long, so you can always go there for a refreshing moment on a hot day. This is the shortest trail in this guidebook, but also one of the most scenic. You can also combine both trails here for a longer hike.

The turnoff to Blanchard Springs is located just east of the community of Fifty-Six (between Big Flat and Sylamore on Hwy. 14). There are many thousands of visitors a year to this place so everything is well marked. Just follow the signs to the parking area for the spring, then take the boardwalk along the creek to the mouth of the spring.

The spring is actually the underground river that flows through the bottom of Blanchard Springs Caverns. This is one waterfall where you can bring your baby along in a stroller! Our recommendation is that you plan to visit during the winter when you will have the place to yourself. Tour the cave and spend the night in the campground, then go see the spring early the next morning—sometimes when it is cold you can see mist coming from the spring. Oh yea, and not only is the spring and mossy creek a real treat to see, but there is a neat "S" bridge along the way which is pictured on the front cover of this guidebook.

Mirror Lake Loop. Be prepared to get wet on this one. If you don't want to get wet, or the creeks are running high, choose another trail, or just do a short part of this one. Waterfalls, rock formations, a creek crossing, a ghostly old grist mill, and more are what await you on this hike. There is also a wheelchair accessible boardwalk and fishing pier, and a very special spot that only a few folks will ever get to see, even though it is right under their noses!

The turnoff to Blanchard Springs is located just east of the community of Fifty-Six (between Big Flat and Sylamore on Hwy. 14). Enter into the park, pass the Visitor Center road and head down the hill. For wheelchair access curve to the left at the bottom of the hill and take the drive to the right directly before the dump station. Regular parking for this trail is available by turning to the right at the bottom of the hill toward the spring, and then park next to the road on the left by the dam (not too much room!).

Head down the steps toward the dam and TURN RIGHT along the boardwalk. At the end of the boardwalk TURN LEFT onto regular trail. Head upstream for a little ways and then begin uphill. At .2 mile you will head down a steep slope and then curve back to the right and head uphill. At .3 mile you will come to an intersection, make a SHARP right and head up the hillside. You'll curve back to the left and level out. The trail heads downhill and comes to an intersection at .4 mile, TURN RIGHT. You will now be back by the river.

At .5 mile you will come to a set of steps to the right— follow those steps. Directly after the steps you will see more steps to your right, those lead to a parking area, head to your left and back to the stream. The trail comes out to the road and turns left and goes across the bridge. Once across the bridge the trail takes off to your left through the brick wall.

Now you are heading downstream on Mill Creek, look back to your left and notice the arched stone bridge. At .6 mile you will cross a stone walkway and you may want to watch the kids in this area, there is a drop off here. At .7 mile look out ahead and to the left and catch your first glimpse of Mirror Lake, and you'll cross over a couple of little wooden bridges. The dam will greet you at almost 1 mile, continue STRAIGHT ahead into the woods.

The trail is not as well maintained or used through here. Head downhill and look back to your left and you'll see a couple of waterfalls, look across and see the old grist mill. Leaf-off is the best time to hike this trail. A little after 1.0 mile the trail takes a sharp turn to the left, watch for this intersection. Head downhill toward the waterfalls and grist mill. You will come to another intersection, TURN LEFT, and get ready to make a creek crossing. Don't miss this spot—incredible scenery with mist rising up off the waterfall, a huge cavern cutting underneath the bluff, just spectacular.

Once you are to the creek you will have to cross the best you can. You are aiming for the tall side of the grist mill where the trail picks up again. If it is deep or you can't see the bottom DO NOT CROSS! Rocks are slick, but take your time and have fun with it. Once across the creek go behind the grist mill and walk along the top of the wall, the trail takes off from there and heads up along the bluff. At 1.1 mile there is a neat bluff overhang. After the overhang you will head uphill and you can see the boardwalk up to your left. The trail curves to the left and goes up rock steps and over the roots of cedar trees and up to the wheelchair-accessible parking area. Once at the parking lot TURN LEFT and follow the boardwalk back to the dam.

While you are in this area be sure to stop by the Blanchard Cave Visitor Center and take the time to see the exhibit hall and watch the movie (both free). Cave tours are getting pretty costly, but it is one of the most beautiful living cavern systems in this part of the world. There is also a short, paved wheelchair trail that loops from one side of the parking area there, and also an old road/trail that goes steeply down the hill and connects with the Mirror Lake Loop.

Scavenger Hunt ? What is the name of the family that owned the grist mill?
(Tim lived with their son's family when he worked at the cave in the 1970's.)

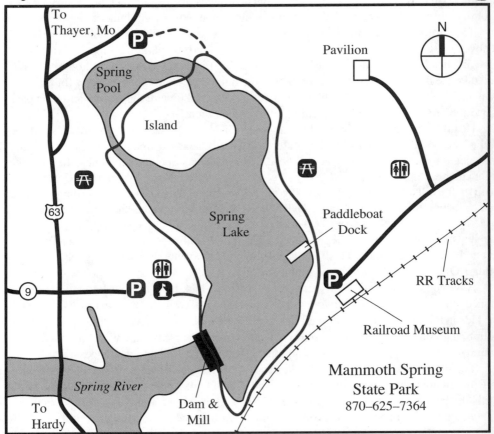

Spring Lake Loop. This loop is paved part of the way. The other part is regular gravel trail that is easy to hike but is not built for strollers or wheelchairs. The trail loops around Mammoth Spring, the 10th largest spring IN THE WORLD. This is an incredibly beautiful and educational area. Pick up a guide at the Visitor Center that explains the numbered points along the trail. Paddleboats are available for rent, there is also a playground and museum. Dogs are allowed but due to the number of geese and other birds, please keep them on a short leash. There is no camping at this park.

To get to Mammoth Springs State Park go two miles south of Thayer, Missouri on Hwy. 63, or 16 miles north of Hardy, Arkansas on Hwy. 63. The Visitor Center is located just off the highway. Park at the Visitor Center and the paved trail begins directly behind the building.

Go behind the building and take the paved trail to the right toward the dam. Once past the dam the trail curves back to the left and eventually heads toward the railroad museum. The paved trail ends there, but the rest of the trail continues off to the left close to the lake through some trees. At this point the trail is no longer stroller accessible. The trail continues around the lake, curves to the left and crosses over a bridge to an island. Explore the island and head out the other end across another bridge. Curve to the left to head back to the parking area and Visitor Center.

Scavenger Hunt ? How much water does Mammoth Spring discharge per hour?

Mossy Bluff Trail
.9 mile round trip

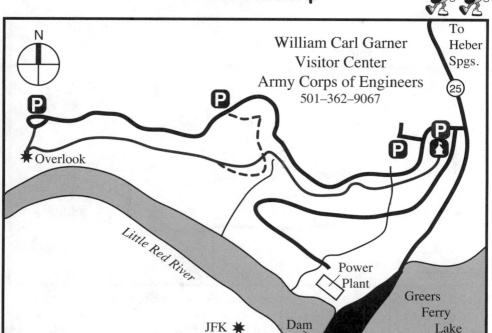

Mossy Bluff Trail. The Mossy Bluff Trail is located just off Hwy. 25 on the west end of the Greers Ferry Dam near Heber Springs.

Park at the William Carl Garner Visitor Center and the trail takes off into the woods at the front of the building. The trail heads down the hill fairly close to the highway. There are numbered posts along the way so you may want to stop in at the Visitor Center and pick up a guided brochure. At a little less than .1 mile you will reach your first bridge. Be careful when it's wet, it will be slippery. The trail curves around, goes downhill and into a powerline right of way at a little over .1 mile. You'll see a road off to your left, continue STRAIGHT ahead into the woods on the other side. At post #7 the trail curves to the left and heads downhill again. At .2 mile you will come to post #8, the trail curves back to the right, look to your left and see the balancing rock. The trail climbs up next to a barbed wire fence and you can see how the trees have actually grown around the fence. The trail curves to the right and heads uphill. You will come to an incredible wooden bridge and rock area at .3 mile. This is a great place to take a break. Directly after the bridge you will come to an intersection, TURN LEFT. About 30 feet after this intersection, you will come to another intersection, TURN RIGHT. You will be taking the Upper Loop, the Lower Loop can be explored as well. The Upper Loop stays fairly level and continues STRAIGHT ahead. Another intersection appears at .5 mile, continue STRAIGHT ahead. The trail comes up next to a beautiful weeping bluff and at .7 mile you will come to a set of steps. Hang on to the younger kids through here. Okay... take a drink of water, are you ready, set, go!

This is an in and out trail so head back the way you came or go up to the overlook area, which is on your left or TURN RIGHT to head out to the parking area and then back to the Visitor Center on the road.

Scavenger Hunt ? How many steps are there at the end of this trail?

Josh Park Memorial Loop
1.2 miles total

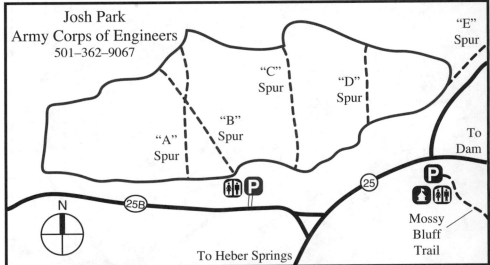

Josh Park
Army Corps of Engineers
501–362–9067

"E"
Spur

"C"
Spur

"D"
Spur

"B"
Spur

"A"
Spur

To
Dam

N

25B

25

Mossy
Bluff
Trail

To Heber Springs

Josh Park Memorial Loop. For an easy stroll through a beautiful forest and a bit of exercise try the fitness trail close to Heber Springs by Greers Ferry. From the Greers Ferry Visitor Center turn left on Hwy. 25 and the next right is Hwy. 25B. Turn right here and Josh Park Memorial Trail will be on your right. There are restrooms and a water fountain here.

You will begin the trail heading to the left. Be sure to breathe deep through here, it's a wonderful pine smell and you are actually walking through an old pine plantation. There are several trails that loop through here and you can mix and match to get the desired length that you want. You are going to travel around the outside loop. There is a trail that takes off to the right at less than .1 mile. Continue STRAIGHT ahead. The trail curves to the right and away from the highway at .2 mile. Another trail takes off to the right at .4 mile, continue STRAIGHT ahead. Shortly after will be another trail taking off to the right, curve to the left. We call this the life preserver tree at .5 mile. See if you can find it (it's to your left). At .6 mile another trail takes off to the right, you will curve left. The trail, up to this point, has been fairly level, now it curves to the right and begins downhill. Another trail "D" takes off to your right and if you need to shorten the hike you can do so here, otherwise continue STRAIGHT ahead. The trail curves to the right and shortly after comes to a trail that takes off to your left, CURVE RIGHT. Another intersection appears at .9 mile. Curve to the left and then curve to the right and head uphill. At 1.1 mile you will see a trail take off to your right, continue STRAIGHT ahead. Shortly after this you will be back at the parking area.

Heat from forest fires cause pine cones to open up and release their seeds. That's one way new forests are born.

Collins Creek Trail
1.0 mile round trip

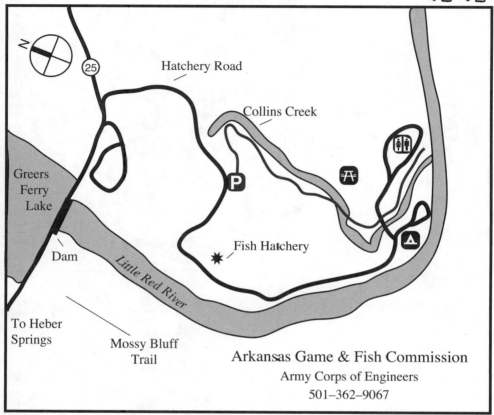

Hatchery Road

Collins Creek

Greers Ferry Lake

P

Dam

Little Red River

Fish Hatchery

To Heber Springs

Mossy Bluff Trail

Arkansas Game & Fish Commission
Army Corps of Engineers
501–362–9067

Collins Creek Trail. Just north of the dam in Heber Springs on Greers Ferry Lake sits a treasure of a trail. From Heber Springs take Hwy. 25 north across the dam and turn right onto Hatchery Road. The trailhead is just .4 mile further on the left. Fishing is allowed.

The trail takes off to the left of the parking area on a gravel path and pretty quickly you begin to hear the waterfall. Just after 400 feet you come to Collins Creek and a waterfall is to your left, the trail curves to the right and follows the creek on its way to meet the Little Red River. Be sure to watch for the "N" tree, which is a tree that has had something interrupt it's growth pattern and in the process of growing around the object, has formed an N. There are plenty of chances to dip the toes or fingers in to Collins Creek. At .3 mile there is a play area across the creek with picnic facilities. Shortly after the play area you will cross a bridge and continue up the hill. At .4 of a mile you will come to a road and cross to the other side. This portion of the trail is stroller accessible and leads you to several fishing piers and the confluence of Collins Creek and the Little Red River. If there is flooding in the area, the lower portion of the trail may be closed. To return to the trailhead, simply turn around and return the way that you came. There is camping available in the area.

Ricketts Mountain Rock Formation
Right next to your car

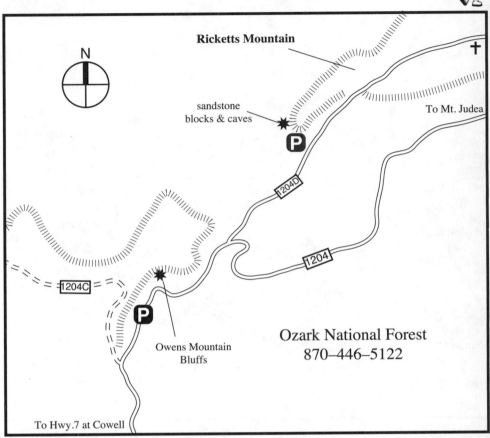

Ricketts Mountain

sandstone
blocks & caves

To Mt. Judea

1204D

1204

1204C

P

Owens Mountain
Bluffs

Ozark National Forest
870–446–5122

To Hwy.7 at Cowell

Ricketts Mountain is one of the most unique rock formations you will ever see, and they're only 100 feet from your car! This is a rock climbing area that few people know about, but since you enter at ground level it is generally safe for kids, although be careful if you let them climb up on top of the rock formation. There is no "trail" here. There are a series of sandstone boulders along the base of the bluff with caves and overhangs all over the place, plus you can make your way up through a split in the bluff and find "turtle rocks" up there, and also a great sweeping view of the sunset, and in the winter, of the sunrise too.

To get to Ricketts Mountain, go east on FR #1204/CR #55 from Cowell (located 17 miles south of Jasper on Hwy. 7) for 5.9 miles TURN LEFT on FR#1204D at the sign for Ricketts Mtn. Cemetery. Go .4 mile and pull in to the LEFT and park at the base of the bluffs.

Notes:

River Valley Region Trails

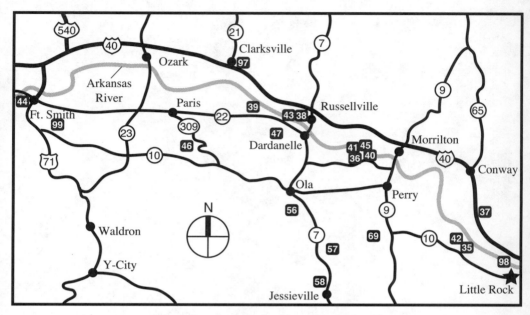

Where are the trails in this region located?

Arkansas Game & Fish Commission
        Bell Slough Wildlife Management Area
        Janet Huckabee Arkansas River Valley Nature Center
Arkansas State Parks
        Lake Dardanelle
        Mount Magazine
        Mount Nebo
        Petit Jean (4)
        Pinnacle Mountain (2)
National Park Service
        Ft. Smith National Historic Site
U. S. Army Corps of Engineers
        Lake Dardanelle (2)
Other
        City of Little Rock
        Town of Little Rock

Trail #	Trail Name	Hike Mileage	Difficulty*	Page #
35	Arkansas Arboretum Loop (Pinnacle Mtn. SP)	.6+	E	83
36	Bear Cave Loop (Petit Jean SP)	.3	E	76
37	Bell Slough Wildlife Loop (Bell Slough WMA, Mayflower)	2.3	M	80
38	Bona Dea Loops (Lake Dardanelle, Russellville)	.1–3.5	E	73
39	Bridge Rock Loop (Lake Dardanelle, Shoal Bay)	.6	M	71
40	Cedar Creek Loop (Petit Jean SP)	1.2	D	78
41	Cedar Falls Trail (Petit Jean SP)	2.0	D	77
42	Kingfisher Loop (Pinnacle Mountain SP)	.5	E	82
43	Meadowbrook Loop (Lake Dardanelle SP)	1.0	E	74
44	River Walk (Ft. Smith National Historic Site)	1.2	E	68
45	Rock House Cave Trail (Petit Jean SP)	.3	E	79
46	Signal Hill/High Point Trail (Mt. Magazine SP)	1.0	E+	70
97	Spadra Creek Trail (Clarksville)	2.8	E-M	72
47	Summit Park Loop (Mt. Nebo SP)	1.8	D	75
98	The Big Dam Bridge (Arkansas River, Little Rock)	1.6	M	84
99	Wells Lake Trail (Janet Huckabee Nature Center, Ft. Smith)	.7	E	69

* on the kid's scale:
E—easy
M—medium
D—difficult

Crickets will tell you the temperature:
Count their chirps for 60 seconds.
Subtract 40 from that total.
Divide by 4, then add 50.
The number you get will be close to the
actual air temperature!

Forget all that cricket math—if you get cold, put on
your jacket. If you get hot, take it off.

River Walk
1.2 miles round trip

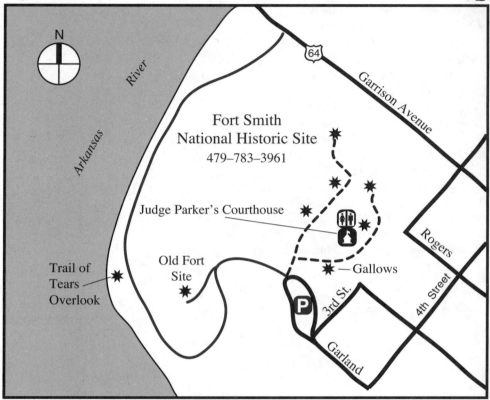

River Walk. A complete education awaits you at the Ft. Smith National Historic Site, not only about the hanging judge, Isaac Parker, but also about the Trail of Tears. While our description does not go into the trail around the old gallows, jail and courthouse, we highly recommend that you experience this part of Arkansas history. There is a small fee to tour the jail and courthouse, but it's worth it.

To get to the National Park head towards downtown Ft. Smith and follow the signs. You can either park at the main parking area, or a block farther on down on Third Street, which is where the River Walk Trail begins.

From the 3rd Street parking area on the south side of the gallows area the trail takes off to your left on pavement. There is a sign there and immediately you will cross over some railroad tracks. Don't forget the bug spray! At less than .1 mile you will come to an intersection, TURN LEFT. Before you do though, walk on out and see the first Ft. Smith. There are benches and interpretive signs along the way. At .3 mile you will come to an overlook on the Arkansas River. The trail continues along side the river. This trail goes out and back, and at .6 mile the trail comes to an end under the highway. Turn around and head back the same way you came in. If you are hiking this in the summer be sure to check out the little shelter area at the beginning of the trail. It has a mister that will rain down cool water on you.

Scavenger Hunt ? **How many people did Judge Parker hang?**

Wells Lake Trail
.7 mile total

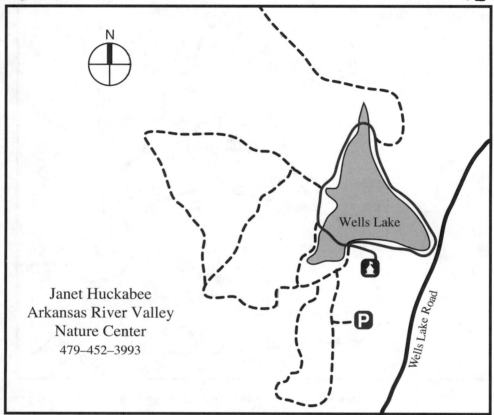

N

Wells Lake

Janet Huckabee
Arkansas River Valley
Nature Center
479–452–3993

Wells Lake Road

Wells Lake Trail The trail system at the Janet Huckabee Arkansas River Valley nature center can be mixed and matched to achieve any skill level or energy level your kids might have. We will only be discussing the Wells Lake Trail here. The nature center is worth a visit but keep in mind that they keep funny hours so be sure to call first to make sure they are open. They are closed on Mondays. The trails are open and can be accessed from dawn to dusk.

The Wells Lake Trail takes off from the back side of nature center or can be accessed by the Wells Lake parking area. From the back of the nature center we head to the left and follow the paved trail. Watch out for the geese and the poo they leave behind. This trail is completely stroller and wheelchair accessible. Follow the pavement, crossing over several boardwalk bridges and curving around the lake. Various trails take off from the Wells Lake Trail so explore to your hearts content. Be sure to bring your fishing pole.

To get to the center from I-40, take the Fort Smith/Van Buren exit #7 onto I-540. Go south 11 miles to exit #11, Zero Street (Hwy. 255), turn left onto Zero Street. Travel just over 4 miles, and turn right on Veterans Avenue. Turn right at the first stop sign, on Frontier Road. Follow Frontier Road, which turns into Wells Lake Road, approximately 2 miles. The Nature Center and Wells Lake will be on the right.

Signal Hill/High Point Trail
1.0 mile round trip

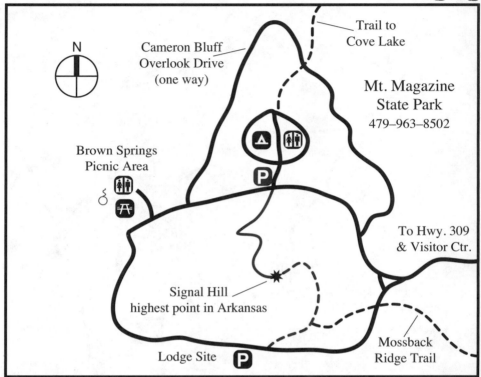

Trail to Cove Lake

Cameron Bluff Overlook Drive (one way)

N

Mt. Magazine State Park
479–963–8502

Brown Springs Picnic Area

To Hwy. 309 & Visitor Ctr.

Signal Hill highest point in Arkansas

Lodge Site

Mossback Ridge Trail

Signal Hill/High Point Trail. What a neat feeling when you are standing on the highest point in the state of Arkansas. It's no Mt. Everest but it gives you a sense of accomplishment none the less. The Signal Hill Trail will take you to that very spot and there is even a registration box there so you can sign your name and let the world know that YOU DID IT!

The park is located on Scenic Highway 309, 17 miles south of Paris; or 10 miles north of Havana. The Visitor Center is a must-see and don't forget to pack the camera.

If you are coming from Paris go to the Visitor Center and turn right. After leaving the Visitor Center go 1.4 miles and turn right, head toward the Signal Hill/High Point Trail. On the sign it may only say High Point Trail. At 1.9 miles from the Visitor Center you will park on the right at the entrance to the Cameron Bluff Campground. Again, the sign says High Point Trail. The trail begins across the road to your left. The Signal Trail goes up 153 feet to the high point. It is a wide beautiful little trail but is not stroller accessible unless you have the heavy duty jogger-type stroller and don't mind pushing *uphill*. The trail does head up but it is not too bad. Once it seems to level out somewhat you will see a road of sorts go off to the right, stay to the left on the trail. Continue to the top, once there you will see the registration box, plenty of benches and a huge sign to have your picture taken by.

When you get ready to leave be sure to take the trail off to your LEFT as you're facing the sign. Return the same way you came in. And be HAPPY, it's all downhill from here......

Scavenger Hunt ? How tall is the highest point in Arkansas?

Bridge Rock Loop
.6 mile total

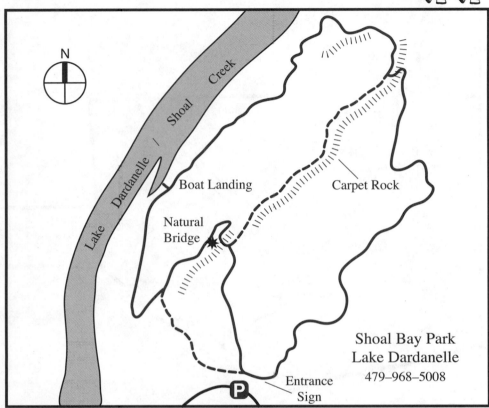

Shoal Bay Park
Lake Dardanelle
479–968–5008

Bridge Rock Loop. A great, short but scenic trail. There is a little bit of climbing involved, but it's worth it! The trail is located in Shoal Bay Park on Lake Dardanelle between Paris and Dardanelle, just off of Hwy. 22. From New Baine, go north on Hwy. 197 for three miles to the Park entrance and turn right.

Begin your hike on the trail that heads off directly behind the big sign. It quickly comes to an intersection at .1 mile—TURN LEFT and head down the hill. This area is a major scenic spot, and you'll find the trail's namesake here—a wonderful sandstone natural bridge. Spend some time here. The trail continues on below the bridge, and comes to another intersection—TURN RIGHT. The trail leads down the hill and to the right, and heads to the lake. At .2 mile, it comes to a boat landing, which makes this trail accessible from the lake. It continues along the lake, past a beautiful rock garden, a good view of the lake. Then at .3 mile it turns to the right, passes the first of several benches, and heads up the hill—all of this area for a while is incredible! And I do mean UP. There are several flights of steps as you climb up through the moss and lichen covered rocks.

At .4 mile there is an intersection—TURN LEFT and continue up the hill. (The right fork takes you on over to "Carpet Rock," another great area, and beyond to the Natural Bridge.) Just a little more climbing, another bench, then the trail levels out—there are some really nice big pines here. It winds on around through the forest, and eases on down a little, back to the parking lot at .6 mile.

Spadra Creek Trail
2.8 mile total

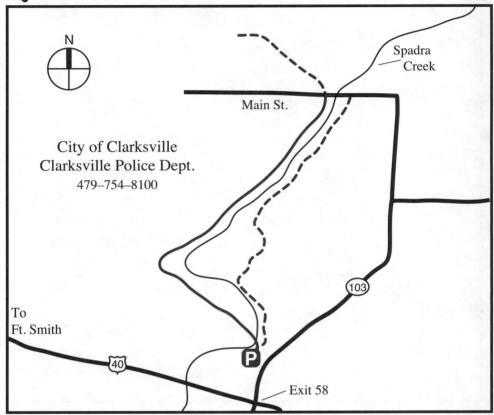

N

Spadra
Creek

Main St.

City of Clarksville
Clarksville Police Dept.
479–754–8100

103

To
Ft. Smith

40

P

Exit 58

Spadra Creek Is accessed from the Iron Bridge between Wendy's and McDonald's at I-40 exit #58, at Clarksville. This trail has two parts with one being stroller and wheelchair accessible and the other being a regular trail. The trail on the east side of Spadra Creek will need to be for your discretion as to whether or not your child is ready and should not be attempted if the water level is high. The east side trail takes off to the right down a very steep flight of steps BEFORE you cross the Iron Bridge. For our purposes we will discuss the stroller accessible trail.

The stroller accessible portion of Spadra Creek begins by crossing the Iron Bridge and following the pavement all the way into Clarksville. There are benches, picnic tables and trash cans along the way. This is a perfect place for the kids to even bring their bikes to ride. After passing a building on your right you will continue straight ahead toward the Main Street Bridge. At this point you can either cross the bridge (hang on to the kids, very busy bridge with lots of traffic) and head back on the nature portion (which is not stroller accessible) or just turn around and go back the same direction.

Bona Dea Loops
.1 to 3.5 miles

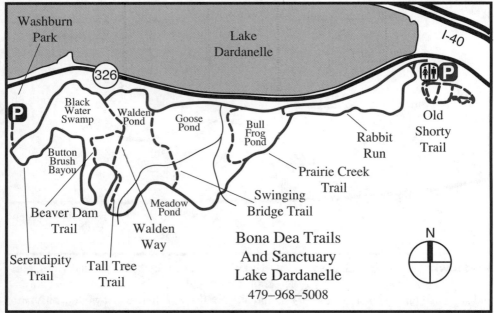

Washburn Park

Lake Dardanelle

I-40

326

Black Water Swamp

Walden Pond

Goose Pond

Bull Frog Pond

Rabbit Run

Old Shorty Trail

Button Brush Bayou

Prairie Creek Trail

Beaver Dam Trail

Meadow Pond

Swinging Bridge Trail

Walden Way

Bona Dea Trails And Sanctuary Lake Dardanelle
479–968–5008

Serendipity Trail

Tall Tree Trail

N

Bona Dea Loops. This is one of Arkansas' most unique trail systems. It's a fitness trail. It's a jogging trail. It's a nature trail. It's a hiking trail. It's a wildlife watching trail. It's barrier free. And it's all within the city limits of Russellville. The U.S. Army Corps of Engineers built this as a multiuse trail, and it has certainly lived up to it. The park covers 186 acres of wetland and low woods, which provide one of the most productive ecosystems found anywhere. It's a wildlife sanctuary for numerous species of animals and especially birds (with an emphasis on waterfowl). The Corps has a booklet available that tells about some of the wildlife that you'll find along the trail, plus information on the fitness stations (get at Arkansas River Visitor Center).

There are several different trails in the park, and you can combine them for many different lengths of hikes/runs/strolls. The longest route is the Serendipity Trail, which runs along the outer edge of the park, and is 3.5 miles long. There are 18 exercise stations along the Rabbit Run and Prairie Creek Trails. Some trails are paved.

Although any time of day is great to visit this park, early morning is a special time here, because you'll be able to see the most animal/bird activity then. The park is also great for bird photography.

I-40 and head towards Russellville, TURN RIGHT at the first light, which is Hwy. 326, and you'll find the park just down the road on the left. (you can also access the trail from Washburn Park at the western end of the trail system via a steep spur trail).

Little cereal boxes make great snacks that you can throw into your backpack.

Scavenger Hunt ? Is there a drinking fountain for dogs here?

Meadowbrook Loop
1.0 mile total

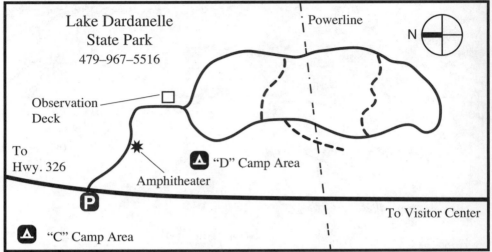

Lake Dardanelle
State Park
479–967–5516

Powerline

N

Observation
Deck

To
Hwy. 326

Amphitheater

"D" Camp Area

P

To Visitor Center

"C" Camp Area

Meadowbrook Loop. A flat, easy trail to hike, with lots of thick and tangled vines, but lots of flowers along the way to see. The trail is wide and flat, but the tread can get soft and soggy so only jeep-style strollers should attempt this one. There is a wonderful Visitor Center at this park—be sure to stop and spend an hour or two there at this state of the art facility! (fish tanks and all sorts of educational and fun things)

To get to the park take Hwy. 326 out of Russellville to the park entrance. Turn right into the park, then take the first left and you'll find the trailhead on the left just a short ways down the road. Continue on this road to get to the Visitor Center. There is lots of camping available, rental bikes, and swimming in Lake Dardanelle.

The trail begins across the road from the trailhead—follow the trail to the Amphitheater, then continue out the other side and into the viney woods. Stay to the right and follow the level trail to an observation deck that you come to on the left. Just past this there is a small bridge, and then an intersection at .2 mile—TURN RIGHT here (you'll return from the left in a little while).

The trail remains level and comes to another intersection at .3 mile (a cutoff trail)—continue STRAIGHT, then across a small bridge to another trail intersection—once again continue STRAIGHT AHEAD (the trail to the right goes out into an open field). You'll pass underneath a powerline, then come to another low bridge across a small creek, and then to another intersection (the second cutoff trail)—once again remain STRAIGHT.

Soon the trail will curve around sharply to the LEFT and begin to head back in the general direction that you just came from. You'll pass the opposite end of the second cutoff trail, then go under the powerline again, then pass the first cutoff trail, and finally wind up back at the end of the loop at .8 mile—TURN RIGHT and go back past the observation deck, then to the Amphitheater and finally to the parking area at 1.0 mile. Remember to go visit the Visitor Center!

Summit Park Loop
1.8 miles total

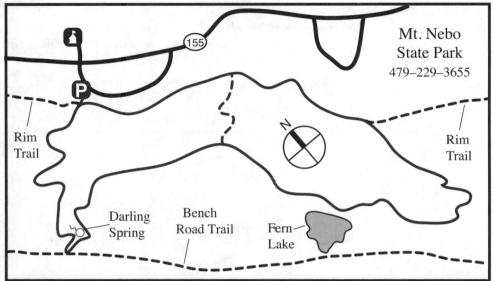

Mt. Nebo
State Park
479–229–3655

Rim Trail

Rim Trail

Darling Spring

Bench Road Trail

Fern Lake

Summit Park Loop. Mt. Nebo State Park sits atop the majestic mountain that rises 1800 feet out of the Arkansas River Valley near Russellville. There are a lot of spectacular views and geological formations along the many trails there. Besides a campground, there are many cabins at the park, and since there are terrific sunrise and sunset viewpoints, you should plan to spend the night. A parking fee may be required.

To get to Mt. Nebo, take exit 81 off of I–40, go south on Hwy. 7 through Russellville to Dardanelle, turn right onto Hwy. 22 west, then turn left on Hwy. 155 south—the last couple of miles up to the top are very steep and winding—not recommended for a large RV on a hot summer day. Turn right once you get into the park and stop at the Visitor Center.

This interpretive trail plunges steeply down the hill past lots of geological formations, springs, a lake, and a multitude of natural things for you to look at. There is a brochure available at the Visitor Center that is keyed to the interpretive points along the trail. To get to the trailhead from the Visitor Center, simply go across the road from it, down the park road there for a couple of hundred yards and you'll come to the parking area on the right. The trail takes off on the right, drops down the hill and to the left. It switchbacks on down past lots of neat stuff, on down to the Bench Trail, then back uphill to the left, and on over to Fern Lake. From there it heads steeply back up the hill, past some amazing rock gardens, up to the Rim Trail, then turns left and follows it back to the parking area. Be sure to take your time along this trail as the rocks can be slick and the hillside is steep. Pack plenty of water and snacks on this one. The views are incredible (especially during the winter), but we recommend this for the family with older kids that have hiked before.

The next four trails are all located at Petit Jean State Park, which is not only one of the best State Parks in the entire United States, but is also a terrific hiker-friendly park for folks of all ability levels looking for great scenery. You can easily spend an entire weekend exploring here, or even longer. Be sure to stop by the Visitor Center for complete details. The park is located on top of Petit Jean Mountain, which overlooks the Arkansas River between Russellville and Morrilton, take either Hwy. 7 from Russellville or Hwy. 9 from Morrilton and follow the signs. One tip—get up early and watch the sunrise over the river from Petit Jean's grave site—it is often quite spectacular!

Bear Cave Loop
.3 mile total

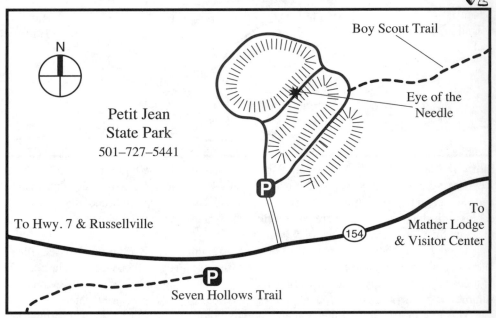

Bear Cave Loop. No, there are not bears on this trail and there aren't any true caves either, but there are some incredible rock formations and plenty of places to explore. The Bear Cave Trail was named after the legend that the last remaining bear on Petit Jean Mountain was killed in this area. The trailhead is located on Hwy. 154 just west of the Lodge area.

You will start the hike directly behind where you park and head up into the rocks on the right. This spectacular area is worth spending some time at, and exploring all of the hidey places. You will soon go between two huge boulders, then you'll come through the slit in those rocks and it will look like the trail turns to the left—continue STRAIGHT ahead. Go past the next boulder and then TURN LEFT. Watch for blazes, take your time and explore. You will start downhill and follow the next big boulder down to your right. Do you feel like you're in a maze? It's all A LOT of fun! At .1 mile you will come to an intersection and TURN LEFT. Follow the blazes. If you look to your right the blazes are a different color than what you have been following. After turning left you will head downhill and curve to the left again. Directly in front of you is the eye of the needle. Great, cool area to have a snack. The trail curves back to the right and down steps. It levels out and follows along the base of the bluff. At .2 mile the trail turns to the left and heads up some steps. At .24 mile you will come to an intersection, TURN RIGHT to go back to the parking area or TURN LEFT for a bit of exploring.

Cedar Falls Trail
2.0 miles round trip

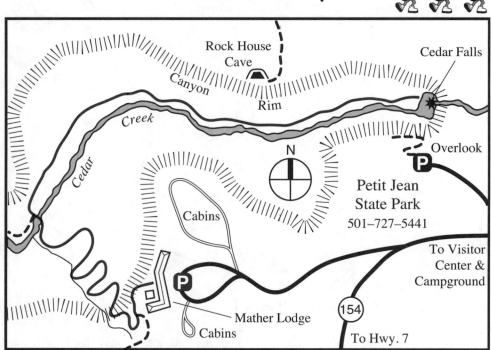

Cedar Falls Trail. This is one of the most used trails in the state, and with good reason, since it takes you to one of the most impressive waterfalls in this part of the country! The area is also an ecological garden—lots and lots of neat plant life. The trail begins at Mather Lodge. It drops on down a steep hill, crosses Cedar Creek, then heads upstream to the waterfall. There is lots to see all along the way. *One word of caution*—the last part of the hike out is pretty tough, and is not recommended for anyone with problems climbing hills. This is a true three-hot-dog trail for kids!

The trail begins through the archway at the Lodge, with a spectacular view out in front of you visible right off the bat. It goes to the left, around and below the swimming pool. Just beyond the pool there is a trail intersection—go RIGHT and head down the hill.

As the trail switchbacks down through giant boulders and next to a tumbling stream, make sure that you stay on the trail—there are lots of opportunities to short cut, which as you can see has caused quite a bit of damage in the past. This entire hillside area is just beautiful. Especially when there is water in the stream! See if you can spot the brightly–colored lichens on the rocks. There are some nice big pines around as the trail finally hits bottom, levels out, and comes to the bridge across Cedar Creek at .35 mile.

Once across the bridge, TURN RIGHT and head upstream. The hike upstream is an easy one, with magical areas at almost every turn—the creek is wonderful, the steep hillside on the left has several boulder fields or "rock glaciers," and numerous large oaks and sweetgum trees tower overhead. Soon you should begin to hear the rumbling of Cedar Falls. This is truly one of the best scenic spots in Arkansas—the wide falls pour 90' into a large pool of water. (No swimming). The trail ends here, and after an hour or two of taking it all in, you should head back out the same way that you came in. Take it easy and go slow back out.

Cedar Creek Loop
1.2 miles total

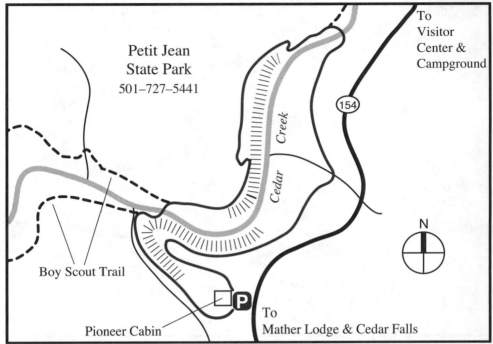

Petit Jean
State Park
501–727–5441

Cedar Creek

154

To
Visitor
Center &
Campground

N

Boy Scout Trail

Pioneer Cabin

P

To
Mather Lodge & Cedar Falls

Cedar Creek Loop. My, oh, my, this is a beautiful trail to hike! It is steep and rocky and not for little fellows, but if you are up to the adventure, you will love this trail. There are a lot of steps going down, and they can get slick. The trailhead is located right on Hwy. 154 between the Visitor Center and the Lodge at an old Pioneer Cabin.

The trail takes off to the left side of the cabin, and soon comes along side a tumbling, rocky creek that is filled with little cascades. It is steep going down with lots of steps so watch your feet! Nice boulders and blufflines all around you. At .2 mile the trail comes to the bottom of this mini-canyon and intersects with the Boy Scout Trail at the edge of Cedar Creek—TURN RIGHT and head upstream, right next to a low bluff that is covered with ferns and mosses. Goodness what a wonderful spot! Just ahead there is a footbridge across the creek—go across it and head up the other side to another trail intersection. Once again TURN RIGHT, and you will begin to climb up away from the creek area, but you will soon level off and be hiking along looking down into the Cedar Creek Canyon.

There are a couple of tight switchbacks up to your left, then the trail is level again, but soon it will cut to the right and make a quick and rocky descent back down to the valley floor. The trail then continues upstream along the creek—all of this area is really spectacular! Soon there is another trail intersection at .6 mile—TURN RIGHT and remain near the creek (the Boy Scout Trail heads uphill). This next short stretch goes across a solid layer of rock and underneath a giant boulder that is leaning up against a bluff! At the far end of it all you will climb up to the end of a second bridge—TURN RIGHT and cross the creek.

Once on the other side the trail curves back to the right and begins a gradual climb out of the canyon, eventually levels off, and winds through the woods just below the highway, which is up on your left. The trail will veer over near the edge of the canyon a time or two for some great leaf-off views, then swing back over near the highway again. It swings around and crosses a small stream right at the 1.0 mile point.

Just as the trail begins to make a sharp curve to the left and uphill, there is one last scenic spot off on the right—a boulder garden and view down into the canyon, but don't get too close! From there the trail heads on up the hill and returns to the old Pioneer Cabin for a total hike of 1.2 miles.

Scavenger Hunt ? How many windows and doors are there in the Pioneer Cabin?

Rock House Cave Trail
.3 mile round trip

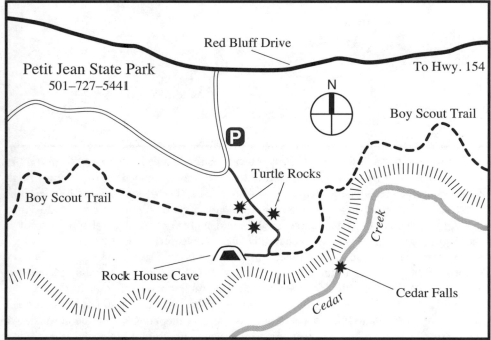

Rock House Cave Trail. This trail is just fascinating and I heard several "This is the coolest place ever!" "Awesome," "Sweet," and much more along the way. Especially at the cave. There are Indian drawings in the center, toward the back and to the left a little. To get to the trailhead from the Visitor Center, head towards the Lodge on Hwy. 154, then turn right and follow the road out to Red Bluff Drive and look for the sign.

The trail begins down a set of steps at the far end of the parking area, and comes to a place known as the Turtle Rocks—hum, I wonder how they got that name? Cross the Turtle Rocks area (follow the blazes) and head towards a directional sign. The trail TURNS RIGHT and heads down a set of steps and comes to another intersection. TURN RIGHT and the cave/overhang is just around the corner. To return to the parking area go back the same way you came in.

Scavenger Hunt ? Why are the Turtle Rocks named Turtle Rocks?

Bell Slough Wildlife Loop
2.3 miles total

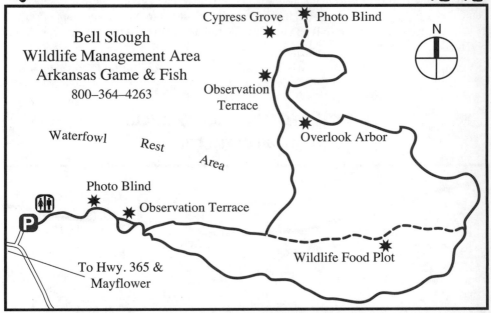

Cypress Grove ✳ Photo Blind

Bell Slough
Wildlife Management Area
Arkansas Game & Fish
800–364–4263

N

Observation
Terrace

Waterfowl   Rest

Area

Overlook Arbor

Photo Blind

Observation Terrace

P

To Hwy. 365 &
Mayflower

Wildlife Food Plot

Bell Slough Wildlife Loop (aka Kenny Vernon Bell Slough Nature Trail). If you like ducks and other waterfowl, this is a great trail for you! It loops around the edge of an official "Waterfowl Rest Area" where thousands of waterfowl and other wildlife can be seen from the trail, and from specially-constructed photo and observation blinds. The trail is easy hiking (but rated two hot dogs due to the length), but one note of warning is that the area often floods a couple of times a year and the trail is inaccessible during those times.

To get to the trailhead, take exit #135 off I-40 at Mayflower, then head south on Hwy. 365 through Mayflower. Continue south out of town and turn left onto Grassy Lake Road, which will take you under the interstate, and finally turn left and park at the trailhead.

There are several different ways that you can utilize this trail. You can make a quick hike out to the first photo blind if you don't have much time; continue on the north side of the loop that hugs the waterfowl rest area to the second photo blind (a round trip of about 1.5 miles); or make the entire outer loop, which is what we are going to do.

From the trailhead the trail crosses several boardwalks and soon comes to the first photo blind/observation point. There is a great view out into the rest area from there. Follow the trail to the next observation area nearby, still along the edge of the rest area. Just past this spot the trail actually goes out onto a roadbed—both the roadbed and trail are surfaced with the same material so make sure you stay on the trail and not the road! The trail crosses the road and then splits—the left fork swings out to the north and to the second photo blind, but you are going to take the RIGHT FORK that heads up a little hill and make the entire loop in a counter-clockwise direction.

The trail levels out and meanders through a nice forest, all of it easy hiking. It curves back to the left and comes to an intersection at .8 mile with a short-cut trail back to the trailhead (it goes past a wildlife food plot)—CONTINUE STRAIGHT ahead. After the trail crosses a small foot bridge, it curves back to the left and climbs up a hill. At 1.2 mile there is an observation arbor on the left. Lots of wildflowers up on this hill, as well as some great views of the surrounding countryside.

From the arbor the trail heads down off of the hill back to the right, then levels out and swings back to the left, where it comes to the intersection with the spur trail out to the photo blind at 1.5 miles. It is just a short hike down to the blind. Back on the main trail, continue STRAIGHT AHEAD as the trail curves back to the left, past a grove of cypress trees that you can see out in the rest area to the right.

The trail runs near the edge of the waterfowl rest area and then heads into the woods again and intersects with the short-cut trail at 1.8 miles—TURN RIGHT and follow the trail back to where the loops come together at the old roadbed. Cross the road and take the trail back past the original photo blind and over the boardwalks to the trailhead, making the total loop of 2.3 miles. If you just did the South Loop (using the cut-off trail), the distance would be about 1.3 miles, and the North Loop would be 1.8 miles. There may be additional trails added so be on the lookout for new intersections.

This fine trail was built from funds received through the special 1/8th cent sales tax, and is one of many "Watchable Wildlife" projects that is constructed and maintained by the Arkansas Game and Fish Commission. **UPDATE:** The wildlife management area and trail were recently renamed in honor of longtime game and fish employee Kenny Vernon, who did a great deal to care for and develop this special place—thanks Kenny!

An owl cannot move its eyes. It must turn its head to watch a moving object.

 Always keep a grown-up in sight. If you are ahead make sure to stop and look back.

Armadillo is Spanish meaning "little armored one."

Kingfisher Loop
.5 mile total

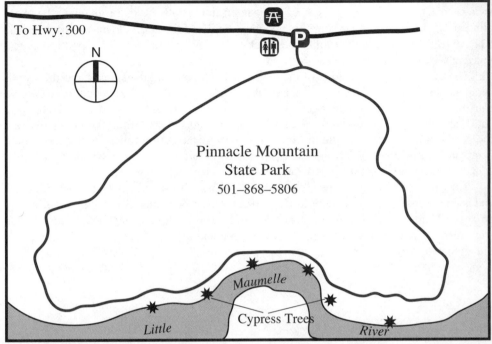

To Hwy. 300

N

Pinnacle Mountain
State Park
501–868–5806

Maumelle

Cypress Trees

Little

River

Kingfisher Loop. WOW!!! That's all we can say about this trail. Grab the bug spray and get hiking! Everyone will love this trail if they are 2 or 102. There are a number of great trails in this park that is located just outside of our Capitol city of Little Rock. Many folks come to hike/run the steep trail up to the summit of Pinnacle Mountain, or spend a quiet afternoon among the cypress knees. The Visitor Center has lots of activities all year long, and some great exhibits.

To get to the trailhead go west from Little Rock on Hwy. 10, turn right on Hwy. 300, go 2.1 miles to the Picnic/Pavilion area and turn right. This is the West Summit Picnic area. Park in the first available parking lot on your right directly after the playground. The Kingfisher Trail takes off into the woods and is paved.

Pinnacle Mountain is directly behind you and if you are up for more of a challenge, well, there you go. But for the rest of us...the trail takes off from the Kingfisher Trail sign to the right. The entire hike is level and perfect for the really young ones. At .1 mile the trail curves back to the left. Watch for turtles, snakes and alligators..oh my! At .2 mile you will see the hugest Cypress Trees, some bigger around than our car! Simply amazing! The trail walks along among these giants and there are a few places that have steps leading down to the trees so they can be looked at closer. You are now walking along the Little Maumelle River. At almost .3 mile you will see Cypress Knees off to your right. Shortly after the knees you will come to a bridge. At .4 mile the trail curves back to the left away from the river. At .5 mile the trail comes back into the open by the parking area and curves to the left to take you back to the beginning of the trail.

Scavenger Hunt ? Do cypress knees grow up and become trees?

Arkansas Arboretum Loop
.6 mile total

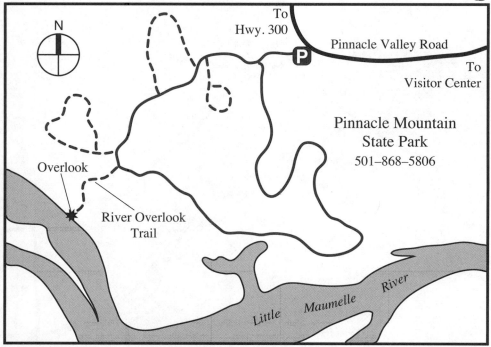

N

To
Hwy. 300

Pinnacle Valley Road

To
Visitor Center

Pinnacle Mountain
State Park
501–868–5806

Overlook

River Overlook
Trail

Little Maumelle River

Arkansas Arboretum Loop. This paved trail is all about education (and trying to find alligators). This delightful trail is a perfect stroll for everyone, and you will learn something new along the way. The signs along the trail have audio recordings which the kids love. Be sure to stop at the Visitor Center and see their display of live animals.

The trail is located at Pinnacle Mountain State Park. To get to the trail from the Kingfisher Trailhead, get back onto Hwy. 300 and continue on, then turn right on Pinnacle Valley Road and go 1.1 mile to the trailhead which is on your right.

Be sure to make a note to yourself that this trail is closed after 5:00 pm in the winter. The trail takes off to the right of the parking lot. Shortly after you start the trail you will see two benches and a water fountain (it even has a doggy water dish too). At the water fountain you will come to an intersection and you need to stay to the right. There are information signs along the way and trails that take off to the right and to the left. These are lesser trails (that are not paved), feel free to check them out, otherwise follow the paved trail. At .2 mile you will come to a lesser trail that takes off to the right, the sign says River Overlook, be sure to check this one out. As you set on the benches overlooking the river, be quiet and watch for ALLIGATORS! The trail meanders through the forest and curves back to the left away from the river. At .6 mile you will be back to the original intersection with the water fountain. Turn right to head back to the parking area.

The Big Dam Bridge Trail
1.6 mile round trip

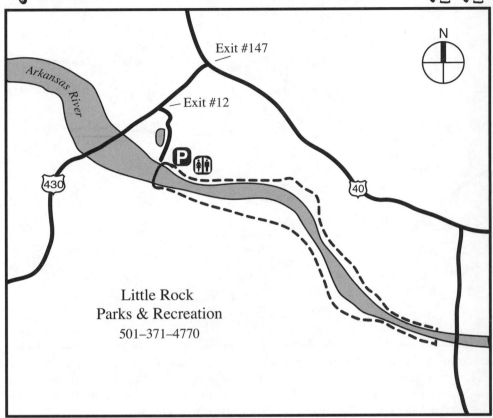

The Big Dam Bridge. The River Trail is a planned 24 mile trail extravaganza located in the Little Rock area. With intertwining paved trails, people will have many options to walk, jog or bike their way around the city. For the purpose of our dayhikes for kids, we will just focus on the Big Dam Bridge, which is the longest pedestrian bridge in the world. This adventure will provide plenty of exercise and learning experience for the kids. Bicycles are allowed if the kids would really like to get in some exercise. It is pretty obvious where you go, just head over the Big Dam Bridge, which at the very peak you will be 90 feet above the Arkansas River.

From I-40 take I-430 south, Exit #147. Take Exit #12, Hwy. 100 towards Maumelle, turn left at that light onto Hwy. 100 East. Turn right at the second stop light onto North Shore Drive. Take the next right onto Cooks Landing Road and you will see a sign for The Big Dam Bridge. As you approach the dam, swing to the left to The River Trail. There are restrooms available and doggy bags to pick up after your puppy.

Notes:

Southwest Region Trails

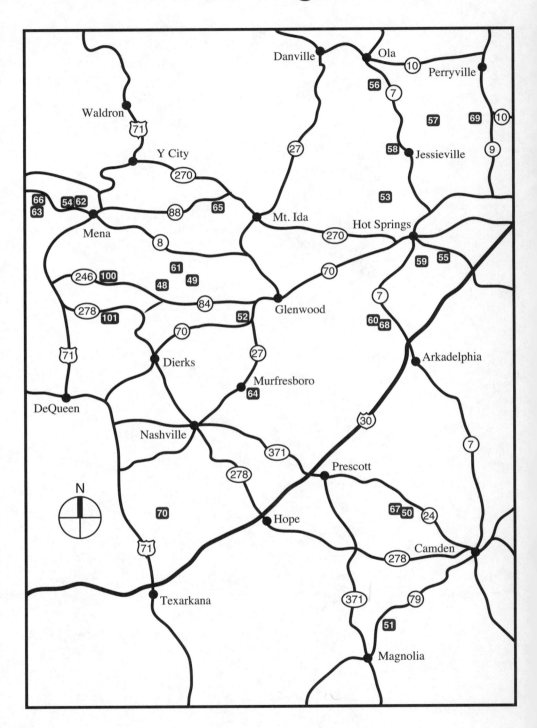

Where are the trails in this region located?

Arkansas State Parks
- Cossatot River (2)
- Crater of Diamonds
- Daisy
- DeGray (2)
- Lake Catherine
- Lake Ouachita
- Logoly
- Millwood
- Queen Wilhelmina (2)
- White Oak Lake (2)

Ouachita National Forest
- Albert Pike
- East End Visitor Center (2)
- Flatside Wilderness
- Jessieville Visitor Center
- Lake Sylvia
- Little Missouri Falls Picnic Area
- Oden Ranger Station
- Shady Lake

U. S. Army Corps of Engineers
- Lake Nimrod

Other
- Garvan Woodland Gardens

* on the kid's scale:
  E—easy
  M—medium
  D—difficult

Trail #	Trail Name	Hike Mileage	Difficulty*	Page #
48	A Valuable Forest Loop (Ouachita National Forest, Shady Lake)	.6	E+	106
49	Bluff Mountain Loop (Ouachita National Forest, Albert Pike)	1.6	D	104
100	Brushy Creek Trail (Cossatot SPNA)	.5	E	109
50	Coastal Plains Loop (White Oak Lake SP)	3.0	M+	112
51	Crane-Fly Loop (Logoly SP)	.7	M	111
52	Daisy Creek Nature Trail (Daisy SP)	.8	E	101
53	Dogwood Loop (Lake Ouachita SP)	.5	E	98
54	Earthquake Ridge Loop (Talimena Scenic Drive)	2.1	M+	90
55	Falls Branch Trail (Lake Catherine SP)	1.4	E+	100
56	Forest Hills Loop (Lake Nimrod, River Road)	1.9	M+	94
57	Forked Mountain Falls (Flatside Wilderness, USFS)	1.6	E	93
58	Friendship Int. Loop (Ouachita National Forest, Jessieville VC)	.9	E	97
59	Garvan Woodland Gardens (Hot Springs)	.25–1.3	E	99
60	Island Loop (DeGray Lake SP)	1.0	E	102
61	Little Missouri Falls (Ouachita National Forest, Little Mo. Falls)	.3	E	105
62	Orchard Loop (Talimena Scenic Drive)	.4	E	90
63	Reservoir Trail (Queen Wilhelmina SP)	.9	M	88
64	River Loop (Crater of Diamonds SP)	1.3	E	107
65	Serendipity Loop (Ouachita Nat'l. Forest, Oden Ranger Station)	1.0	E	92
66	Spring Trail (Queen Wilhelmina SP)	.7	E	89
67	Spring Branch Loop (White Oak Lake SP)	.3	E+	113
68	Towering Pines Loop (DeGray Lake SP)	.6	E	103
69	Trees of the Forest Loop (Ouachita National Forest, Lake Sylvia)	.6	E	96
70	Waterfowl Way Loop (Millwood SP)	1.5	E	110
101	Waterleaf Trail (Cossatot SPNA)	.2	E	108

Reservoir Trail
.9 mile round trip

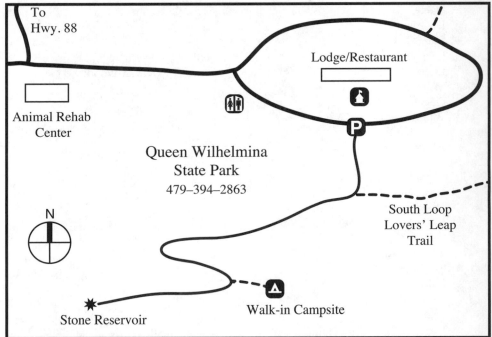

To Hwy. 88

Lodge/Restaurant

Animal Rehab Center

Queen Wilhelmina State Park
479–394–2863

N

South Loop Lovers' Leap Trail

Walk-in Campsite

Stone Reservoir

Reservoir Trail. To get to Queen Wilhelmina State Park, from Mena travel northwest for 13 miles on Hwy. 88, Talimena National Scenic Byway. The views are spectacular along this road so be sure to pack the camera. After entering the park the next road on your left goes to the Lodge and Visitor Center. The trail begins across from the entrance to the lodge (the big round part of the building), down a set of boardwalk steps and turns to your right. There are plenty of trails at this park so you can mix and match and come up with trails that are just right for you. This particular trail has a lot of steps, which can get slick when wet, so beware!

After you have turned right you will cross an open field and head into the woods. This is another trail at this park that is perfect for wildflowers. Coneflowers, sunflowers and more! At less than .1 mile the trail turns to the left and heads down some steps. Once down the steps, it curves to the right and levels out. At .3 mile the trail curves to the right (do not go into the walk-in campsites, there is a sign there). The views through here will be delightful during leaf-off. At .4 mile you will reach the old stone reservoir which was built in 1898 to supply water for the hotel located above. They used an old steam engine to pump the water to the top of the hill. This is an out and back trail so turn around and head back the way you came in. This trail may not be very long but the climb out can be kind of steep.

The average raindrop falls at 14 miles an hour, which is the speed of a slow car.

Spring Trail
.7 mile round trip

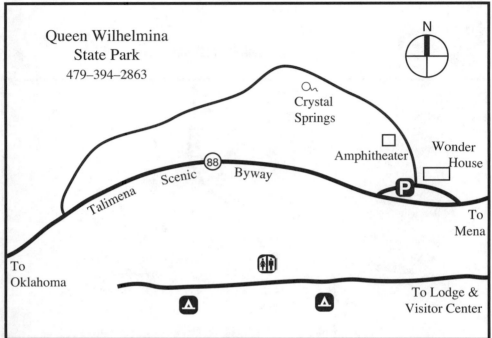

Queen Wilhelmina
State Park
479–394–2863

N

Crystal
Springs

Amphitheater

Wonder
House

88

Scenic   Byway

Talimena

P

To
Mena

To
Oklahoma

To Lodge &
Visitor Center

Spring Trail. We have not seen this done on a trail before but what a simply wonderful idea, a silhouette trail. Along this hike kids can watch for the shapes (silhouettes) of local wildlife. Don't worry, they're just cut outs, but it is still neat to see what you can find along the way.

To get to Queen Wilhelmina State Park, from Mena travel northwest for 13 miles on Hwy. 88. After entering the park the next road on your left goes to the Lodge and Visitor Center and the next road on your right is the parking for the Spring Trail. Parking is located at the Wonder House and if you have a chance be sure to check it out. The Wonder House is a nine level house.....WOW!

The Spring Trail begins between the Wonder House and the Amphitheater. Head into the grassy area and immediately down some steps. All along this trail the wildflowers are stunning. Wild sunflowers, purple coneflowers, horse mint and the list continues. In the summertime the trail is dense with lush flowers but in the winter when the leaves are off, it will be the views that will capture your attention. At less than .1 mile you will reach Crystal Spring. Directly after the spring you will head up some steps. At .3 mile you will cross a little wooden bridge. At almost .4 mile you will reach the main road and at this point you have a choice—either turn around and go back the way you came or walk the road back to your car (which is what we did). The right of way on both sides of the road is wide and shouldn't create a problem walking back to your car. When you get up to the road TURN LEFT and follow the road back to the Wonder House.

Earthquake Ridge Loop
2.1 miles total

Orchard Loop
.4 mile total

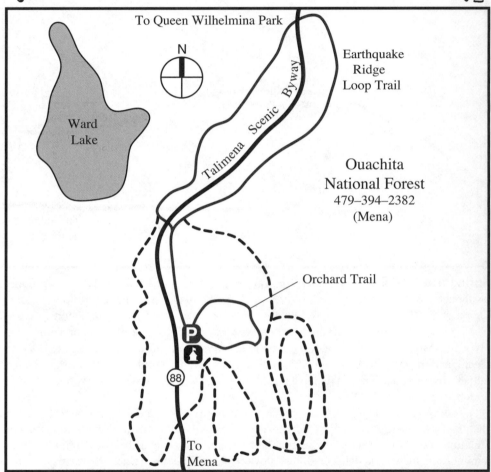

To Queen Wilhelmina Park

N

Ward Lake

Talimena Scenic Byway

Earthquake Ridge Loop Trail

Ouachita National Forest
479–394–2382
(Mena)

Orchard Trail

P

88

To Mena

Earthquake Ridge Loop. This short loop trail is one of many that are located at the East End Visitor Center of the Forest Service, which is just west of Mena on Hwy. 88 up on the Talimena Scenic Byway (this is different from the Forest Service District Office, which is on Hwy. 71 in Mena). The Visitor Center is open much of the year, but may be closed in the wintertime. This trail is popular with mountain bikers.

The trail is blazed with white paint, and takes off from the parking area into the pine woods on the level, next to the highway. It comes to a trail register (please do), and splits—your're going to take the LEFT FORK. It swings on up to and across the highway , then switchbacks up a hill, and the views behind get better with every step. It finally levels off and straightens out. There are some nice hardwoods, then at .6 mile the trail intersects a jeep road—TURN LEFT on the road and run along it for just a hundred feet or so. After a while the trail heads up the hill, at times steeply, and passes some rock gardens along the way. It tops out at about 1.0 mile.

It heads on down the hill to and across the highway (when I hiked this there were fresh bear tracks in the trail). The trail drops some, but not too steeply. During leaf–off there are some great views out across the way. It passes a couple of nice rock gardens, lots of big pines, and at 1.6 miles, a small spring. The hillside is very steep, but the trail does its up–and–downing on a pretty gentle grade. It eventually does head up the hill to the registration spot, which completes the loop at 2.0 miles—TURN LEFT and head back to the trailhead.

Orchard Loop. There is an entire trail system of short loops located at the East End Visitor Center. There are so many trails that it could easily overwhelm you, and there is a little bit of something for everyone.

The Orchard Trail is one of the best, and is a level, paved trail that is stroller and wheelchair accessible the entire way. There are interpretive signs along the way that tell about the history of the land and this area. When you pull into the Visitor Center pull around to the second parking area and you are going to start the paved trail leading to the left. The trail meanders through huge pine trees and is just wonderful. At .2 mile you will come to a boardwalk leading off to the left that goes out to a neat little rest area. At .3 mile you will see a trail that heads off to the left, follow the paved trail curving to the right. You will see another trail head off to your left, just be sure to stay on the paved trail all the way back to the parking area.

When the air is dry (fair weather), pine cones will open up; and when there is moisture in the air (rain on the way?), they will close.

 Holly trees have stickers....watch out.

Deciduous trees (oaks, maples and hickories) lose their leaves in the winter. Evergreen trees (pines, cedars, and spruce) keep their needles all year.

Serendipity Loop
1.0 mile total

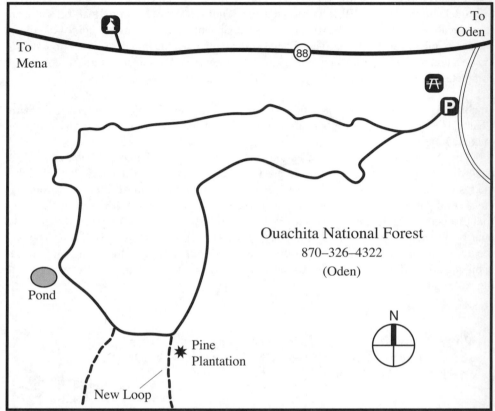

To Mena

88

To Oden

Ouachita National Forest
870–326–4322
(Oden)

Pond

P

N

Pine Plantation

New Loop

Serendipity Loop. This trail is one of the best little interpretive trails around. It's very short, easy to hike, and the signs there interpret the forest like no other trail you'll ever see. It's in the Ouachita National Forest, right across from the Oden District Ranger's Office. Definitely worth a side trip to go see. To get there, take Hwy. 88 west out of Pencil Bluff (on Hwy. 270 near Mt. Ida) to Oden. Go through town 1.5 miles and turn left into the parking lot—the District Office is just down the highway on the right.

The gravel trail heads out past a signboard to the left, then splits—TURN LEFT. One of the signs explains the different "layers" in the forest—a tree layer, vine layer, shrub layer, herb layer, and a forest floor layer. The trail winds around through the forest, passing a number of labeled trees and other stuff. It crosses a small bridge, and passes a bench. There are some giant pine trees here and there, and the rest is a nice open forest.

The "Pine Plantation" spot is at .4 mile, and there is a bench there. The trail swings on around to the right, towards a spur trail to the left at .5 mile that leads down to another bench that overlooks a pond. It continues on around to the right, over a hollow–log culvert, past many more ID signs, and begins to head back to the trailhead. TURN LEFT when you reach the intersection and return to the parking lot, for a total hike of just under one mile total.

Scavenger Hunt ? What does "serendipity" mean?

Forked Mountain Falls
1.6 miles round trip

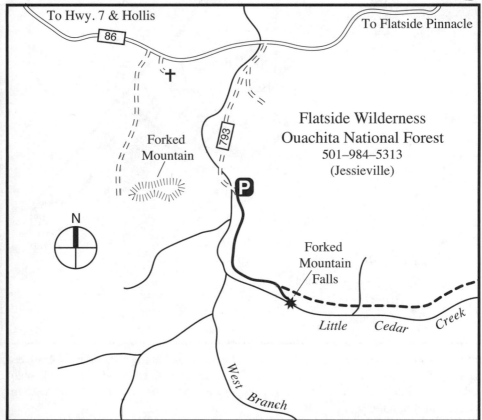

To Hwy. 7 & Hollis

86

To Flatside Pinnacle

Forked
Mountain

793

Flatside Wilderness
Ouachita National Forest
501–984–5313
(Jessieville)

P

N

Forked
Mountain
Falls

Little   Cedar   Creek

West Branch

Forked Mountain Falls. There is a neat little waterfall and pool in the shadow of Forked Mountain that is easy to get to and makes for a wonderful side trip for folks traveling down Scenic Hwy. 7 Byway. It is located inside the Flatside Wilderness Area, where no vehicles or motors of any kind are allowed.

To get to the parking area, take FR#86 (gravel) east from Hwy. 7 (the turn is located just south of Hollis, and north of Jessieville). Go 4.7 miles and turn right onto FR#793. Go .9 mile (cross the creek twice) and park at a locked gate at the wilderness boundary (there is a great rock outcrop looming over where you park).

Hike along the closed road past the gate, up and over a couple of humps. The old road will drop down some and level out, then begin to curve to the left a little bit. There is an old road trace that veers off to the RIGHT at about .7 mile (the first roadbed continues on). This old trace will take you over to Forked Mountain Falls. There is a nice pool of water there—hum, perhaps a quick dip might be in order? One note of warning—the rocks are *very* slick!

As you hike along you can look up over your right shoulder (or out in front of you when you are coming back out) and see Forked Mountain, which is one of the most unique mountains in Arkansas. It has two different but connected peaks, and a giant boulder scree field spilling down the north flank, reminiscent of Rocky Mountain peaks.

For the return trip simply retrace your steps back to the parking area.

Forest Hills Loop
1.9 miles total

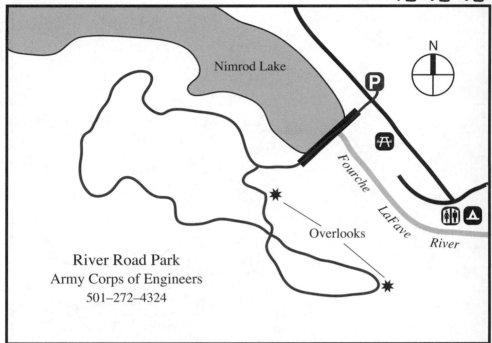

Nimrod Lake

N

Fourche LaFave River

Overlooks

River Road Park
Army Corps of Engineers
501–272–4324

Forest Hills Loop. Here is a great Corps trail that is located at the Nimrod Lake Dam eight miles south of Ola on Hwy. 7. Go through the intersection with Hwy. 60 and it is the second road to your right. Make your way to the parking area above the dam which is about .5 mile once you turn into the park.

The trail begins by going across the dam, where you'll see a hillside of kudzu. Once across the dam veer to the right across the field and head into the woods. (Notice a trail coming down from the left—that is where you will end your hike.) You will see posts along the way with arrows on them. These are not pointing out the direction of the trail, but rather pointing to subjects of the posts. There are plenty of these interpretive signs along the way, as well as HUGE pine trees. The trail heads uphill, levels out and meanders through the forest. There are wonderful views through here during leaf-off. At .4 mile you will head down a set of steps, cross a bridge, and curve to the right. What a beautiful area, especially when the water is running. The trail goes up, levels out, curves to the left and continues on the top of a ridge. There is a very well placed bench in the middle of a tough climb at .6 mile. At .7 mile the trail turns to the right, then starts steeply downhill and you will see partridge berry everywhere. The trail starts uphill again, curves to the left, passes a bench and continues up. You will eventually level out and curve back to the left. Pass a bench at the 1.0 mile point, curve to the right and head up. You did say you wanted a workout right? Soon after the bench you will come to an intersection, continue STRAIGHT ahead. If the kids are tired TURN LEFT at the intersection to head back to the trailhead.

The trail heads uphill and to the right. At 1.2 miles the trail levels out and curves back to the right. Sunrise and sunset are great times to be here, especially during leaf-off. You'll feel like you're on top of the world. On the back side of this ridge you will be walking among

94

Atoka Sandstone outcrops—notice how different it is on this side of the hill. At 1.3 mile the trail begins downhill and curves to the right. The intersection that you came through to begin this loop is at 1.6 mile, continue STRAIGHT ahead, downhill. Shortly after the intersection the trail curves to the left, in front of you is a view of the dam and we are now on top of the kudzu hill. Continue left past a bench and then curve to the right and begin down a steep set of steps. Watch out for the kudzu, it will reach out and trip you. At the next intersection TURN RIGHT and return to the parking area.

Scavenger Hunt ? **How high is the top of the dam above the river?**

The first trees to bloom in the spring are normally serviceberry or "sarvis" trees, not dogwoods.

 Pack extra water and an extra snack.

A fully grown oak can make 50,000 acorns in one season.

Trees Of The Forest Loop
.6 mile total

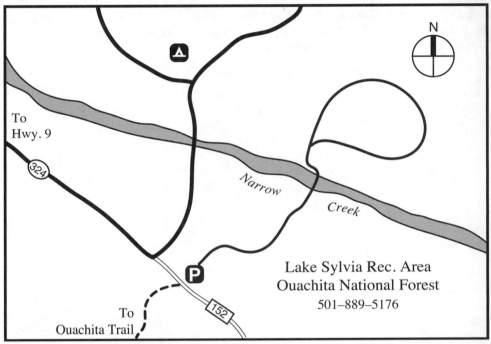

N

To
Hwy. 9

324

Narrow

Creek

P

152

To
Ouachita Trail

Lake Sylvia Rec. Area
Ouachita National Forest
501–889–5176

Trees Of The Forest Loop. To get to the Lake Sylvia Recreation Area go on Hwy. 9 south out of Perryville for 8.2 miles to Hwy. 324. Turn right onto Hwy. 324. Go four miles to the campground. Immediately after the campground the pavement ends and gravel begins, parking is on your left. There is a wonderful little swimming area here and several other trails that you can check out, so plan to spend the day.

Part of this trail is paved and is wheelchair and stroller accessible. From the parking area you will see a sign for the Ouachita Trail that takes off behind the sign, you will begin on the paved trail between the two wooden fences. This hike is fairly level for the paved part and there are interpretive signs along the way that are also written in braille. At .1 mile you will come to a boardwalk bridge. At .2 mile you will come to another boardwalk bridge that crosses a beautiful little stream. The trail then curves to the left and shortly after the pavement ends. From this point on the trail is hard packed gravel but is not wheelchair or stroller accessible. At the next intersection continue STRAIGHT ahead. At .3 mile the trail curves back to the right and heads downhill. At .4 mile you will be back at your original intersection, TURN LEFT to go back to the parking lot.

Bananas are not good snacks to carry in your packs. They smush easy.

Friendship Interpretive Loop
.9 mile total

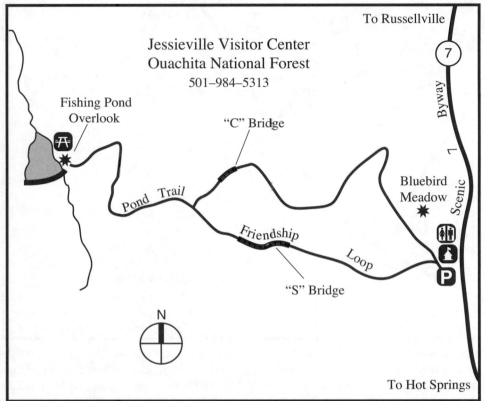

Jessieville Visitor Center
Ouachita National Forest
501–984–5313

To Russellville

7

Byway

Scenic 7

Fishing Pond
Overlook

"C" Bridge

Bluebird
Meadow

Pond Trail

Friendship

Loop

"S" Bridge

N

To Hot Springs

Friendship Interpretive Loop. This is a beautiful little trail that is paved and is barrier free. It loops around through the woods behind the Forest Service Visitor Center at Jessieville. Take your lunch with you and stop at one of the many benches or picnic tables and enjoy some time outside. To get there, go north on Hwy. 7 about 18 miles from Hot Springs. The Visitor Center is on the left just outside of Jessieville. You should go inside and have a look at their deer and other neat things!

You start off heading clockwise (to the left). The trail winds through a nice forest, and past many interpretive signs. Be sure to stop and take a few minutes to read them. It goes across a wonderful wooden bridge that was built in an "S" shape. Not too far beyond the trail forks—take the LEFT FORK, and you'll head on out to the fish pond. The trail turns back to the right, then left, and ends up at an observation point that overlooks the pond (there is an accessible picnic pavilion and bathroom there). All along there are lots of big pine trees and oaks, and wildflowers scattered around too.

From the pond you'll head back to the intersection, then TURN LEFT there and continue around the loop. Next up is the "C" bridge, another nice wooden structure. The trail swings to the right, then left, then sharply right again. It passes Bluebird Meadow as it eases downhill and back to the beginning.

Dogwood Loop
.5 mile total

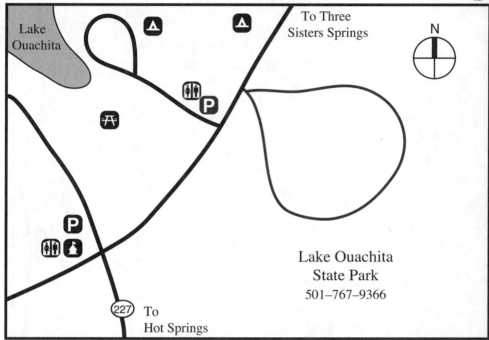

Lake Ouachita

To Three
Sisters Springs

N

Lake Ouachita
State Park
501–767–9366

227 To
Hot Springs

Dogwood Loop. What a delightful trail is all that can be said about this spot. The trail is very well maintained with signs posted along the way. To get to Lake Ouachita State Park from Hot Springs travel three miles west on Hwy. 270 then 12 miles north on Hwy. 227 to the park. After you enter the park you will come to a four way stop, go straight ahead to see the Visitor Center or turn right toward the Three Sisters Spring to go directly to the trailhead. Park at the next road on your left. The trail begins on the other side of the road.

Head into the woods and you will immediately see an arrow pointing to the right, turn to the right and begin up a slight hill. The trail heads uphill just a short distance and levels out. Watch for Quartz (crystal looking) rock. Beautiful, but please leave it for others to enjoy. Shortly you will curve to the left and head up a slight hill. The trail meanders through a pine forest and as the name implies, in the spring will be full of blooming Dogwood trees. The trail does a bit of up and downing and curving through here but nothing too major. At .3 mile the trail curves back to the left and heads downhill. There are some steps through here. You will come to a sign about the Red Fox. Red Fox are normally reddish-yellow and along the trail you will be able to spot a den. The trail will begin a series of "switchbacks" which is a way to get down a hillside going from side to side instead of straight down. This is done to ease the impact on the land and the hiker. Please stay on the trail. Continue down the hillside back to the starting point at the road.

Be sure when you're in this area to visit the Three Sisters Springs. Kids seem to find this fascinating. Each spring was said to have its own healing powers. For instance, Spring #2 makes you go poo and Spring #1 makes you stop pooing. And now the modern medical world has proven that there are indeed different minerals in each spring. Don't drink the water though, it is now polluted.

Garvan Woodland Gardens
.25 to 1.3 mile loops

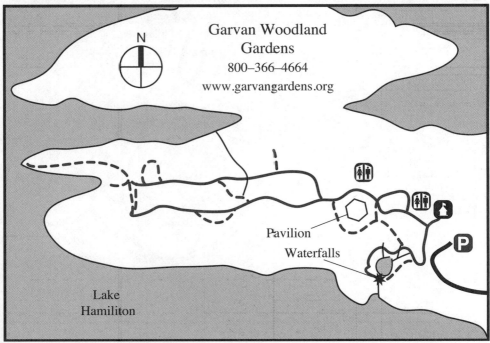

Garvan Woodland
Gardens
800–366–4664
www.garvangardens.org

N

Pavilion

Waterfalls

P

Lake
Hamiliton

Garvan Woodland Gardens Trails. The Gardens are owned by the University of Arkansas, and they have a long and colorful history. Besides the main waterfall and interesting features fashioned with water and stone (including a really neat arched bridge made of stone), there are literally thousands of blooming plants all over the place in the spring and summer (it's pretty darn nice in the fall and winter too!), and many trails that wind through the 210-acre property. And they are building a special Kid's garden too! It is open most days of the year, except for some of the major holidays—call or visit them online for more information (see map above). There is an entrance fee charged but it is well worth every penny. Many of the trails are suitable for strollers and wheelchairs.

To get to the gardens from Hot Springs take the Carpenter Dam Exit (Hwy. 28) off Hwy. 270 bypass and head south for five miles, then turn right on Arkridge Road until you come to the garden entrance. A waterfall is one of the first things you will see if you hike the trail down the hill in a clockwise direction. They built a unique little step-across bridge at the bottom of this falls that is actually two rocks facing each other. With all of the wonderful trails to choose from we couldn't pick just one. Hike them all, have a picnic, or just sit on one of the many benches and watch the hummingbirds and butterflies dance. The entire family will enjoy this place.

Don't approach or touch any wild
animals you might see.

Falls Branch Trail
1.4 miles round trip

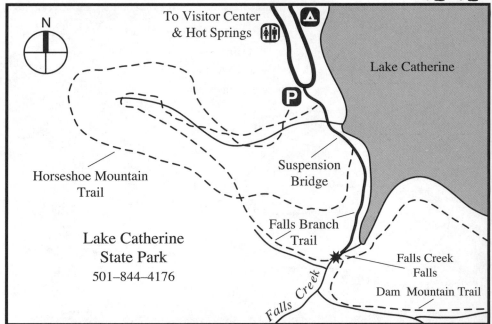

To Visitor Center & Hot Springs

Lake Catherine

Suspension Bridge

Horseshoe Mountain Trail

Falls Branch Trail

Lake Catherine State Park
501–844–4176

Falls Creek Falls

Dam Mountain Trail

Falls Creek

N

Falls Branch Trail. You've probably seen this waterfall in dozens of photographs—it is one of the favorite falls used to advertise Arkansas State Parks. The hike to the falls is an easy stroll along the lake shore. If you are feeling energetic, you can hike several different loop trails that connect with this one for a total hike of 6.3 miles. But we'll just stick with the short hike to the base of the falls and back. By the way, the name of the creek is Falls "Creek" and the waterfall is Falls "Creek" Falls, but the name of the trail is Falls "Branch" Trail.

From Hot Springs, take Hwy. 270 east and turn right onto Carpenter Dam Road (Hwy. 28), then left on Hwy. 290, then left again on Hwy. 171 and follow it all the way into the park. From Little Rock, take I–30 south to exit 97 near Malvern, then go north on Hwy. 171 until you reach the park. The trailhead is located at the back of the park, just past the amphitheater. This is a fully-equipped campground with plenty of sites here, but you may find the constant drone of the powerhouse across the lake a bit annoying.

There are several trails that take off from the trailhead, but the one you want is the Falls Branch Trail that goes down near the lake shore. It heads out through some nice big trees, crosses a road near the camping area, and goes over a foot bridge—you are following the white blazes. (There are actually three different trails that share the first part of this route, so you will see different colored blazes on the trees). The trail begins to follow the lake shore, then at .4 mile crosses a nice suspension bridge. Just beyond it you come to an intersection—continue STRAIGHT AHEAD and along the lake.

Soon the trail curves around to the right and heads up into a small cove, and to the waterfall at .7 mile. The trails continue from this point, one crossing the creek above the falls and looping around a hill and back to the same point, another trail follows a little stream (or "branch") uphill and then eventually back to the trailhead. You can take your pick of them all and spend a good part of your day hiking here, or simply head back the way you came.

Daisy Creek Nature Trail
.8 mile round trip

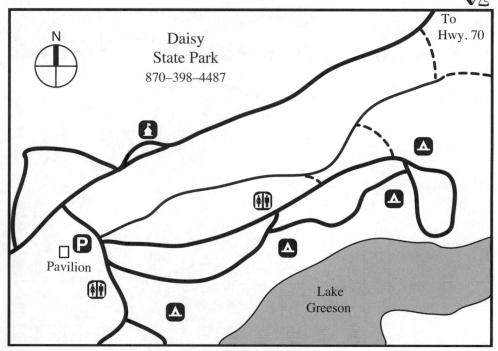

Daisy Creek Nature Trail. To get to Daisy Creek State Park from Hot Springs, travel 50 miles southwest on Hwy. 70 to the town of Daisy. Turn left into the park. The Visitor Center will be on your right .5 mile down this road. Take the next road on your left and park next to the pavilion for the Nature Trail.

The trail begins across the road to the left of the parking lot entrance. The best hiking time will be any time other than the middle of summer. If you happen to be here then, watch for the MILLIONS of tiny frogs along the trail. At .1 mile there is a trail that comes in from the left, curve to the right and look for the trail blazes on the tree (white). There is a large electrical box with a metal fence around it at .2 mile—directly after this electrical area TURN LEFT. Shortly after that you will come to an intersection, TURN LEFT here and head down a hill (there is a house up to the right). At the bottom of this hill you will cross a creek. If there is high water this will be a wet crossing so be prepared. Shortly after you cross the creek you will come to an open meadow area with the lake out to your right. This is beautiful through here, take your time and enjoy.

Stay close to the tree line and head into the trees on the other side. Again, watch for the blazes. After you walk through those trees you will directly come into another open area with the lake still on your right (this is a perfect place for a picnic lunch). Continue across the meadow. The trail comes to a dirt track that is used by motor bikes. At this point, you have a choice, continue exploring on those dirt tracks or turn around and head back the same way you came in.

This trail may not be the most scenic in the world but it is a delightful, level hike to some beautiful lake areas. The kids will enjoy this one. Just watch out for those frogs.

Island Loop
1.0 mile total

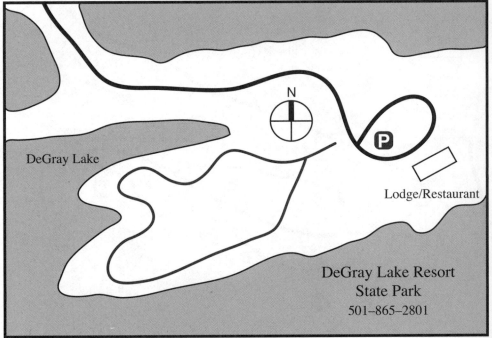

DeGray Lake

Lodge/Restaurant

DeGray Lake Resort
State Park
501–865–2801

Island Loop. Located on the main island of DeGray Lake State Park is a simply delightful trail. It is easy to spend the entire weekend at this State Park or simply take this trail for a gentle stroll after dinner. To get to DeGray Lake Resort State Park take Hwy. 7 north from I-30 (exit 78) just six miles, or, take Hwy. 7 south from Hot Springs about 21 miles to the park entrance.

To begin this trail cross the causeway on to the island and park at the main lodge. The trail takes off to the right of the lodge into the woods on a fairly level walk. The trail is wide and is blazed with orange blazes. Shortly after heading into the woods the trail curves to the right and heads towards a road. At about .1 mile you will come to the road, cross here and head into the woods on the other side. The trail heads off to the LEFT. Throughout this entire trail you will have views of the lake (especially during leaf-off) and will be hiking through beautiful pine forest and hardwoods. This is an extremely peaceful trail meandering along the shore of the lake the entire time and is stunning at sunset. At .4 mile you will come to what looks like an intersection, you need to TURN RIGHT, look for the blazes. At .5 mile you will come to a spectacular view out across the lake, be sure to step back and enjoy this wonderful place that you are in. Shortly after the wonderful view the trail turns back to the right and goes up a small rise. At .6 mile the trail curves to the right and heads away from the lake. The trail wanders back and forth through the woods and at .9 mile you will come to the original intersection, TURN LEFT, cross the road and follow the trail back to the lodge.

Towering Pines Loop
.6 mile total

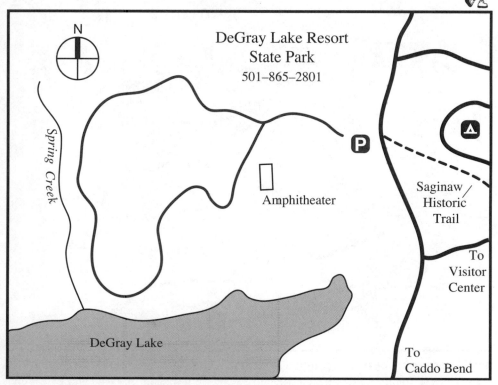

Towering Pines Loop. There are so many trails at this State Park and so little time. All of the trails in this area are family appropriate so please stop in at the Visitor Center and see what else they have to offer. To get to DeGray Lake Resort State Park take Hwy. 7 north from I-30 (exit 78) just six miles, or, take Hwy. 7 south from Hot Springs about 21 miles to the park entrance. Once you pass the park entrance drive 2.3 miles to the Caddo Bend turn off. When you reach the stop sign turn right and go .1 mile to the Amphitheater (which is on the left). Park there and the trail begins straight ahead.

Just after starting the trail, curve to the right and you will see the Amphitheater on your left. This is a wide trail but is not stroller accessible. Shortly after the curve the trail comes to a bridge, narrows and then goes up a hill. At about .1 mile the trail comes to an intersection, TURN RIGHT. After making it up the next hill a gentle stroll through a pine forest awaits you. At .3 mile the trail curves to the left and goes up a hill. The trail curves back to the right and heads towards the lake. Shortly after, the trail curves to the left following the shore line and remains fairly level. At .4 mile the trail curves back to the left and leaves the shoreline. At .5 mile the trail meets back at the original intersection. Turn right to head back to the parking area.

If you stop to take a break, look all around when you get up to go and make sure you didn't forget anything or leave trash behind.

Bluff Mountain Loop
1.6 miles round trip

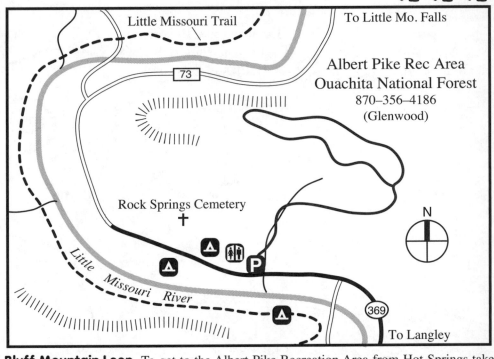

Little Missouri Trail

To Little Mo. Falls

73

Albert Pike Rec Area
Ouachita National Forest
870–356–4186
(Glenwood)

Rock Springs Cemetery

N

Little Missouri River

P

369

To Langley

Bluff Mountain Loop. To get to the Albert Pike Recreation Area from Hot Springs take Hwy. 70 west 36 miles through Glenwood to Salem. Turn west on Hwy. 84 and go 13 miles to Langley. At Langley turn north on Hwy. 369 and go six miles to the recreation area. The trail begins just before the restrooms, next to the Amphitheater.

The trail takes off to the right and crosses over a bridge. Curve to the left and you will come to an intersection. Take the left fork.. The trail crosses the little stream that you have been following at .1 mile. There are plenty of beech, holly and pine trees along this trail, so there will be green to be seen in the winter months. The first part of this trail is uphill but the good news is that on the way back it's all DOWNHILL. At .2 mile the trail crosses a wooden bridge and heads up to your right and away from the stream. The trail comes to a bench and an intersection at .4 mile, TURN RIGHT. At .5 mile the trail switchbacks to the left and begins a steep climb to the top. During leaf-off the higher you go the better the views are. Be sure to take it slow and easy through this area, stop for water breaks. The trail tops out at .7 mile and the view is worth the effort. You will be looking down on the Little Missouri River. Curve to the left and continue along the top of the ridge. A bench awaits your tired legs at .8 mile. Whew.....what a view! Keep going, we're not done yet. The trail continues along and then curves back to the left and heads downhill. At that curve there is a primitive trail that takes off to your right, we don't really recommend kids going there unless they are experienced hikers and climbers. At .9 mile as you are heading downhill be sure to look back to your right and see the neat rock formations. The trail meets up with the original intersection with the bench at 1.2 mile. Continue STRAIGHT ahead and downhill back to the parking area.

Little Missouri Falls
.3 mile round trip

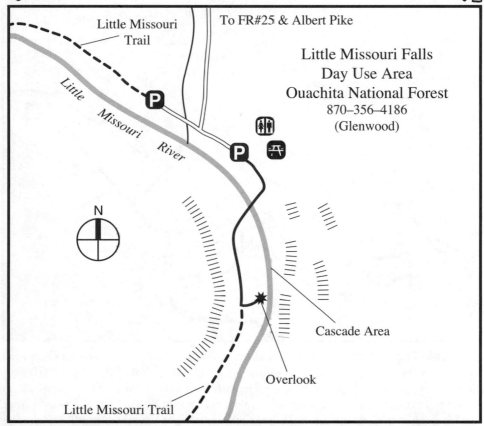

Little Missouri Trail

To FR#25 & Albert Pike

Little Missouri Falls
Day Use Area
Ouachita National Forest
870–356–4186
(Glenwood)

Little Missouri River

P

P

N

Cascade Area

Overlook

Little Missouri Trail

Little Missouri Falls. The whole family will love this spot. There is plenty to do and explore. You can swim in the summertime, or hike far downstream on the Little Missouri Trail. Caution: If the water is high, be careful—never step into water you can't see the bottom of!

From Langley (west from Glenwood on Hwy. 70 and then west on Hwy. 84) take Hwy. 369 six miles to Albert Pike Recreation Area. Continue straight through the campground as the road turns to FR#73 (gravel), and follow it about three miles and turn left onto FR#43. Go 4.3 miles to the intersection with FR#25 (you will have been driving through the Crooked Creek Gorge for the past .5 mile—lots of nice cascades!), turn left onto FR#25 and go .7 mile and turn left at the big sign, which will take you down into the picnic area where you park. From Norman take Hwy. 8 west 12.7 miles and turn left onto FR#43. Go 4.7 miles and turn right on FR#25, then turn right after .7 mile to get to Little Missouri Falls.

The paved trail leaves the parking area and crosses the creek on a brand new bridge and goes to a pair of overlooks with good views of the cascade area. There are small falls and pools all over the place. NOTE: strollers and wheelchairs will be able to go across the bridge to the other side but won't be able to continue on to the overlooks.

Scavenger Hunt ? What name do you recognize on the bronze plaque?

A Valuable Forest Loop
.6 mile total

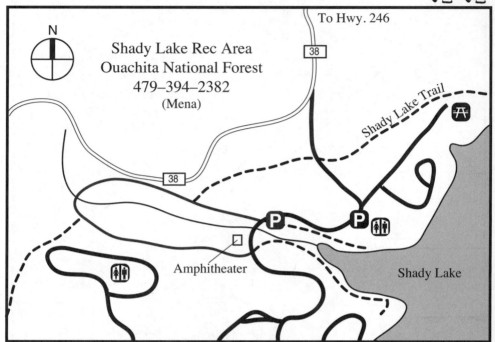

N

Shady Lake Rec Area
Ouachita National Forest
479–394–2382
(Mena)

To Hwy. 246

38

Shady Lake Trail

38

P   P

Amphitheater

Shady Lake

A Valuable Forest Loop. From Hot Springs take Hwy. 70 west 32 miles to Glenwood. Continue on Hwy. 70 through Glenwood four miles to Salem. Take Hwy. 84 (west) out of Salem through Lodi and Langley, to Athens. In Athens take Hwy. 246 to Forest Service Road 38, turn right (north) and travel three miles to the entrance to Shady Lake Recreation Area.

Once you come into the recreation area turn right when you come to a T intersection. Just before you cross a stone bridge parking will be on your left and the trail takes off to the right. There are interpretive signs along the way and for the first part of the hike you will be on an old road bed heading upstream of a little creek. When the water is flowing you'll be in for a real treat. At less than .1 mile the Shady Lake Trail takes off to your right, continue STRAIGHT ahead on the wider trail. The further upstream you go the better it gets with little waterfalls along the way. At .2 mile you will come to a bench that overlooks the stream....simply, wonderful. Shortly after the bench the trail TURNS LEFT, crosses a bridge and TURNS LEFT again. You will be on a large stone path, and at the end of the stone path the Shady Lake Trail takes off to your right, curve to the LEFT and continue downstream on regular trail. Through the springtime the wildflowers will be abundant through this area. The trail gets pretty steep around .3 mile, but don't worry—there is a bench waiting for you at the top. At .5 mile you will see the Amphitheater off to your left, but just keep going STRAIGHT ahead. Soon you will be back to the road, then TURN LEFT and cross the creek to get to your car.

There is a trail on the parking side of the creek that follows the creek to the lake and swimming area. And if you are in the mood for more hiking check out the Shady Lake Trail. At 3.2 miles it is a bit longer and tougher as it goes all the way around the lake, and it's open to mountain bikes.

River Loop
1.3 miles total

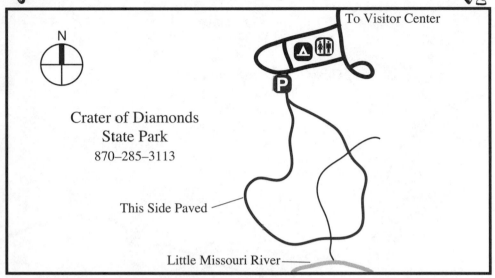

To Visitor Center

N

Crater of Diamonds
State Park
870–285–3113

This Side Paved

Little Missouri River

River Loop. In the mood for a new diamond or like playing in the dirt? What better way to spend the day than hiking in the morning and digging for diamonds in the afternoon. The Visitor Center should be your first stop when you come into Crater of Diamonds State Park. They have an educational film and plenty of displays to teach you what you will be looking for. Just a warning though....it can be EXTREMELY hot out in the diamond field in the summertime so be prepared and pack plenty of water.

Crater of Diamonds State Park is located two miles southeast of Murfreesboro on Hwy. 301. Turn right to go to the Visitor Center or turn left to go directly to the trailhead. You will curve around and go by a dump station. Take the next road to the right. Stay on this road until you come to a parking area on the right, directly after camp site 21. The River Trail is paved for the first .6 mile.

At .1 mile you will see a secondary trail come in from the left—stay on the pavement. The trail meanders through a beautiful forest staying fairly level. At .4 mile the trail curves to the left and the Little Missouri River is on your right, and you are still on pavement at this point. At a little over .5 a mile the pavement ends at an area with a bench that is perfect for relaxing and just watching the river roll by. If you have a stroller or wheelchair at this point you will need to turn around and return the same way you came in. Otherwise the trail turns to the left.

At .6 mile the trail curves to the right, goes down some steps and towards a little creek. Shortly after, it crosses a bridge, and turns to the left away from the creek. At .7 mile you will come to some steps. Through this area take note of the erosion that has occurred. The creek is not all that big but has carved a huge ravine in the land. At .8 mile the trail has come close to the creek again. Watch the kids in this area. The drop-off is not all that big, but watch them anyway. Shortly after you will come to a second bridge. After the bridge the trail curves to the left. At a little over one mile you will come to the intersection with the pavement. TURN RIGHT to head back to the trailhead......and to find your fortune.

BY THE WAY: we left the really big diamonds there for you to find—but beware, all that glitters may not be diamonds!

Waterleaf Trail
.2 mile total

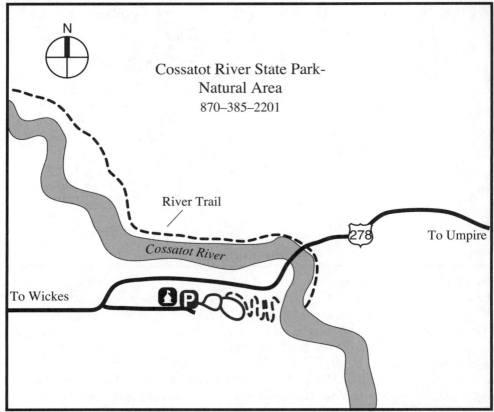

N

Cossatot River State Park-
Natural Area
870–385–2201

River Trail

Cossatot River

278

To Umpire

To Wickes

Waterleaf Trail can be found east of the town of Wickes on Hwy. 278. Go 9.2 miles from the town of Wickes and the Cossatot River Visitor Center is located on the right or South side of the highway. The Visitor Center is a must see for the whole family. With educational information and live animals there is something for everyone. Who knew that scorpions were so common in Arkansas!

The Waterleaf Trail begins to the right of the Visitor Center and is stroller and wheelchair accessible. A playground is at the beginning of the trail for some added playtime, along with picnic facilities. The trail forms a figure eight and has informational signs along the way. On the north side of the trail you will see a trail take off into the woods that is *not* stroller friendly. This trail takes off steeply down the hill and ends at the Cossatot River. The Waterleaf Trail curves back around and ends up back at the Visitor Center.

Brushy Creek Trail
.5 mile round trip

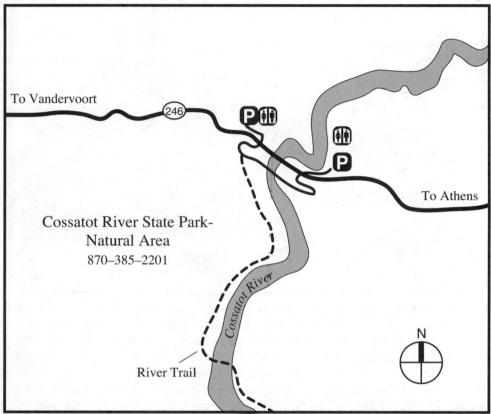

To Vandervoort

246

Cossatot River State Park-
Natural Area
870–385–2201

To Athens

Cossatot River

River Trail

N

Brushy Creek To get to the Brushy Creek Access area go east on Hwy. 246 for 8.2 miles from Vandevoort. There is parking on the north side of the highway before and after the bridge that crosses the Cossatot River. The access area parking after the bridge is a day use only area and has restrooms, picnic facilities, and one of the neatest swimming holes around. We will start our little hike on the west side of the bridge and head to the paved walk that says River Corridor Trailhead.

The trail curves around and goes underneath the highway. Once you come out the other side the trail works it's way up to a pedestrian bridge that crosses the Cossatot River. Beautiful views looking both directions. This bridge actually covers up a gas pipeline and if you are afraid of heights this will not be the place for you. Once to the other side the trail curves to the left and becomes non-stroller accessible heading down a flight of steps. The trail then goes underneath the highway again and meanders along a boardwalk through the woods. You end at the day use area which will allow for picnicking and swimming. Pay attention to the water levels.

Waterfowl Way Loop
1.5 miles round trip

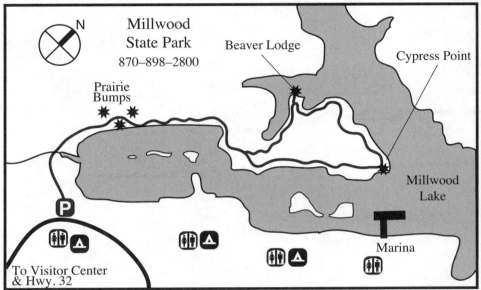

Waterfowl Way Loop. This unique trail at Millwood State Park gives you a rare opportunity to see *alligators*! Plus there is lots of other wildlife to see, like a beaver lodge, and of course a bunch of waterfowl, including blue herons, white egrets, bald eagles, geese, and tons of ducks. The park is located on Hwy. 32 between Ashdown and Saratoga in extreme southwest Arkansas, at the western end of the Millwood Lake Dam. There is a nice campground there, and a marina. An entrance fee may apply. Be sure to check in at the Visitor Center, and pick up a trail brochure, which has descriptions of the 20 interpretive stops along the way.

The trailhead is located at the back of camp area E (near site #97). The best time to hike it is in the early morning or late evening, when wildlife is most active. Go slowly, and quietly, and keep your eyes open! The trail takes off behind the carved wood sign and heads across a foot bridge. A cove of the lake is off on the right–you will follow along the shoreline. It's an easy, level walk through the woods.

The trail veers away from the water a couple of times, but comes right back to the shore-line. There are several resting benches along the way. At .4 mile, near interpretive post #10, there is a shallow ditch—this is actually a "beaver run," where beavers have been traveling between the two bodies of water—you'll see a few chewed trees too! Stay to the RIGHT here (you will loop back to this spot from the left).

The trail continues along towards the end of the cove and the main lake, past an incred-ible area of great pine trees at .6 mile. It comes to a picnic table at the end of Cypress Point, then swings back to the left and heads back into another cove. Two benches on this side are set up as blinds, where you can sit quietly and look for wildlife. At the second one, at .9 mile, there is also a spur trail—this short spur leads over to a *working* beaver lodge! This is a great spot to spend some time (and see alligators?).

From here the trail continues on to the beaver run again at 1.0 mile—TURN RIGHT and follow the trail back to the trailhead, for a total hike of 1.5 miles.

Crane-Fly Loop
.7 mile total

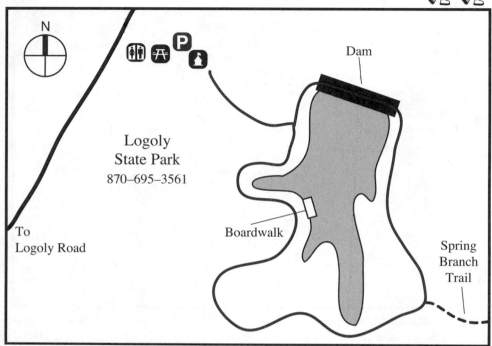

N

Dam

Logoly
State Park
870–695–3561

To
Logoly Road

Boardwalk

Spring
Branch
Trail

Crane-Fly Loop. Logoly State Park is located six miles north of Magnolia on Hwy. 79. Turn on Logoly Road or CR# 47 and the State Park entrance will be on your left. Be sure to stop at the Visitor Center to see the exhibit of snakes and even an alligator or two, and to pick up a brochure to go with the numbers along the trail. If you are hiking this trail in the late spring or summer watch for copperheads that blend in with the pine needles.

The Crane-Fly Trail begins directly behind the Visitor Center and heads down a flight of steps toward a pond. The trail heads to the RIGHT of the pond and past a picnic table. This is a nice gravel trail but it does get steep in places. At .1 mile you will come to a wooden bridge and then curve back to the left. After the wooden bridge you will head up a hill on a flight of steps. Once to the top of the hill turn to the left and head down a set of steps. The trail curves back to the right away from the pond but before you do so, check out the boardwalk out into the pond. At .2 mile the trail curves to the left and crosses a bridge. The trail meanders through the woods curving left and right, up and downing and crosses another bridge. At a little over .3 mile the trail comes to another set of steps. At .4 mile you will come to an intersection, TURN LEFT to follow the Crane-Fly Trail. Shortly after the intersection you will come to a neat little step/bridge thing that goes up and over a dead tree. Directly after that you will head down a set of steps. At .5 mile the trail comes to a wooden bridge then curves up and to the right. The pond is down on your left. The trail curves down and to the right, down some more steps and comes to another bridge at almost .6 mile. As you come to this next intersection and the swinging bridge be sure to look down to your left and watch for turtles, snakes or who knows...maybe an alligator. Once you reach the swinging bridge TURN LEFT to head across the dam of the pond. The trail curves to the left once you cross the dam and heads back towards the Visitor Center.

Coastal Plains Loop
3.0 miles total

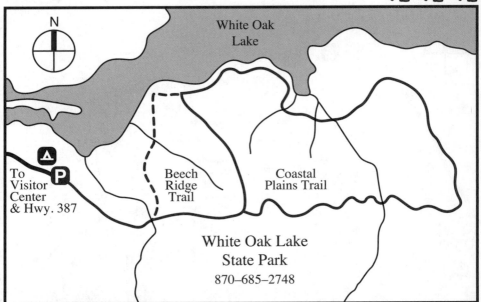

Coastal Plains Loop. This is the first of two trails we'll visit at this great State Park. Besides hiking, there is plenty to do here. Fishing, paddleboats, camping, wonderful programs for the kids, basically, it has it all. To get to White Oak Lake State Park from I-30 at Prescott, travel twenty miles east on Arkansas Hwy. 24 to Bluff City, then take Arkansas Hwy. 299 for about 100 yards before turning onto Hwy. 387, then go 2.5 miles south to the park. Go to the Visitor Center to check out all of their neat programs and learn about the history of this area.

This first loop is actually two trails joined together—the Beech Ridge and Coastal Plains trails, but we'll call it the Coastal Plains Loop. The trailhead is located at the back of the camping area—"E". The trail begins at an archway at the end of the camp area.

The trail heads out on the level and comes to a spectacular area right away—some of the largest pine trees that you'll find on any trail in the state. And then it crosses a long, low wooden walkway that is pretty unique in itself—just a lovely spot. There is another walkway just ahead. Something that is interesting to do when you're around such big trees as these is to go over to one of them, get right up against it, and look up the trunk. Wow!

The trail continues on, crosses a small stream, then heads up just a little. It crosses a roadbed that comes in from the left—continue STRAIGHT AHEAD. You'll notice that the forest has changed dramatically—different trees, different underbrush and ground cover, a totally different environment—partly due to the soil types. It swings around to the left and gradually climbs, coming to a trail intersection at .6 miles—TURN LEFT (you'll return on the trail that comes in from the right).

You're on an old roadbed now, heading down just a little, and the trail is marked with paint blazes. It curves to the right and heads on down to the lake shore. At .9 mile it comes to a "T" intersection—you can take the Beech Ridge Trail back to the left and rejoin your loop, but it's more scenic the other way, so you're going to TURN RIGHT on the old roadbed and hike around the shore of White Oak Lake.

One of the first things that you see are large beech trees on both sides of the trail. And just beyond there is a great view out across the lake. There are a few large pines along here too. The trail winds on around along the lake, and by 1.3 miles has veered away from it some and left the big beeches. It crosses a couple of small streams and passes some larger hardwoods and more big pines, then eases uphill just a little, still on the old roadbed.

At 1.7 miles you come to an open area and begin to skirt around the right edge, then quickly TURN RIGHT and head into the woods, away from the field. It heads back to the right on narrow trail. This is a different type of forest environment still. The trail swings to the left and down, through a beautiful area with a tiny stream and huge beech trees. It runs along the fern–lined, sandy–bottomed creek. At 1.9 miles there is a bench, and a bridge across the creek. This is a small, but wonderful spot, and a good time to take a break and soak it in!

Across the creek the trail begins to head uphill, back to the left and away from the creek. It winds around up the hill, soon leveling off. The forest is more open now, with a grassy floor. At 2.3 miles there is a huge oak tree just on the right—it's not the tallest tree, but it is one of the biggest around. A little ways past this giant at 2.4 miles you reconnect with the loop—GO STRAIGHT AHEAD, and head on down the hill back towards the trailhead.

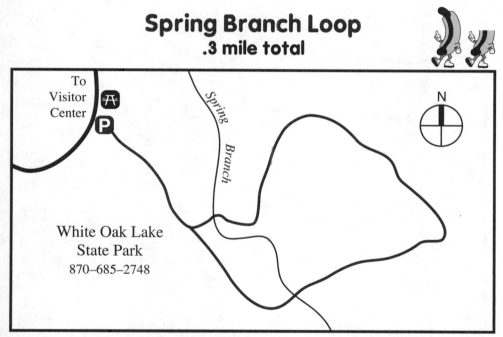

Spring Branch Loop
.3 mile total

Spring Branch Loop. Here is another neat little trail in this same park. Pick up a brochure at the Visitor Center to go along with the numbered posts along the way. To get to the trailhead from the Visitor Center head toward the Picnic Pavilion, on a one-way road. Parking for the trail is on your left.

At less than .1 mile you will come to an intersection with a bridge to the left, continue STRAIGHT ahead. The trail meanders through a pine forest and crosses over the little stream on a bridge. A bit of up and downing and then at .3 mile you will come to a bench that over-looks a little stream. Shortly after the bench you will come to another bridge and cross the stream. You are now back to the original intersection. TURN RIGHT to head back to the parking area.

East Region Trails

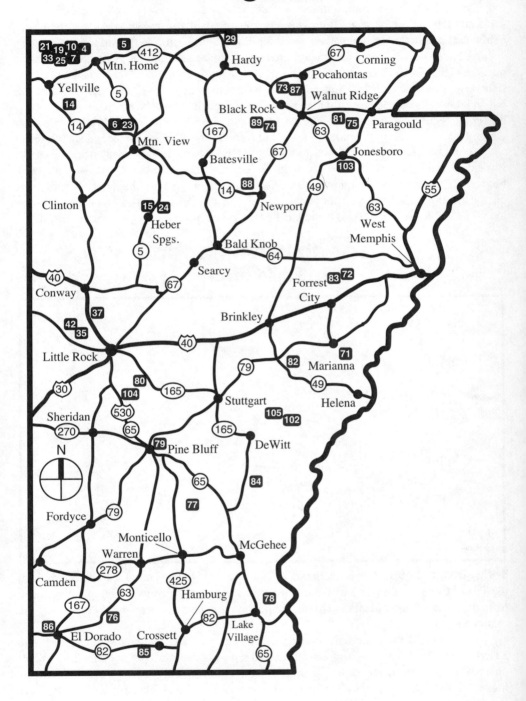

Arkansas Game & Fish Commission
       Delta Rivers Nature Center
Arkansas State Parks
       Cane Creek
       Crowley's Ridge (2)
       Jacksonport
       Lake Charles (2)
       Lake Chicot
       Louisiana Purchase
       Mississippi River
       Moro Bay
       Old Davidsonville (2)
       Toltec Mounds
       Village Creek (2)
Other

       Arkansas Post National Monument
       Felsenthal National Wildlife Refuge
       El Dorado High School
       Lorance Natural Area
       White River National Wildlife Refuge (2)

* on the kid's scale:
E—easy
M—medium
D—difficult

Trail #	Trail Name	Hike Mileage	Difficulty*	Page #
71	Bear Creek Loop (Mississippi River SP, Marianna)	1.0	M	127
72	Big Ben Loop (Village Creek SP)	.5	E+	129
73	Black River Loop (Old Davidsonville SP)	1.1	E+	133
74	Butterflies & Blooms Trail (Lake Charles SP)	.3	E	134
102	Champion Tree Trail (White River National Wildlife Refuge)	2.4	E	125
75	Dancing Rabbit Loop (Crowley's Ridge SP)	1.3	M	130
76	Deer Run Loop (Moro Bay SP)	.4	E	117
77	Delta View Loop (Cane Creek SP)	2.5	M	120
78	Delta Woodlands Loop (Lake Chicot SP)	1.0	E	119
79	Discovery Loop (Delta Rivers Nature Center, Pine Bluff)	.5	E	121
103	Habitats Trail (Crowleys Ridge Nature Center)	.3	E	139
80	Knapp Loop (Toltec Mounds SP)	.8	E	137
81-	Lake Ponder Loop (Crowley's Ridge SP)	.5	E	131
104	Lowrance Creek Trail (Lowrance Natural Area)	.5	E	138
82	Louisiana Purchase Boardwalk (Louisiana Purchase SP)	.4	E	126
83	Military Road Loop (Village Creek SP)	2.2	M+	128
84	Old Townsite Loop (Ark. Post National Monument)	1.4	E	122
85	Periwinkle Loop (Felsenthal Nat'l. Wildlife Refuge, Crossett)	1.5	E+	118
86	South Arkansas Arboretum (El Dorado High School, El Dorado)	.25–2.0	E	116
87	Trappers Lake Loop (Old Davidsonville SP)	.9	E+	132
88	Tunstall River Walk (Jacksonport SP)	1.3	E	136
105	Upland Nature Trail (White River National Wildlife Refuge)	.7	E	124
89	White Oak Loop (Lake Charles SP)	.9	M	134

South Arkansas Arboretum
.25 to 2.0 miles

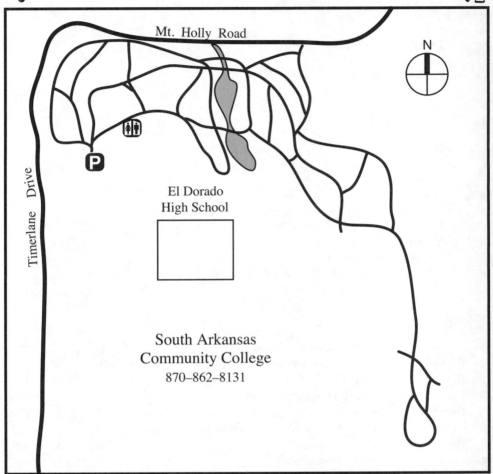

Mt. Holly Road

N

Timerlane Drive

P

El Dorado
High School

South Arkansas
Community College
870–862–8131

South Arkansas Arboretum. A hidden treasure of the El Dorado area. Located just north of the El Dorado High School it is close to everything and yet can seem so remote. The 13-acre Arboretum is managed by the South Arkansas Community College and is simply a delight. The trail is mostly stroller and wheelchair accessible but some of the hills can be a tough push. So be forewarned......

To get to the Arboretum Trail take Hwy. 82B/Hillsboro in El Dorado to Timberlane Drive, go north on Timberlane Drive .6 mile to reach the High School which is located on your right. The trail begins to your left behind a fenced gate. Please be sure to sign in at the registration book. There are restrooms, and a pavilion there so bring a picnic lunch.

There is a maze of trails throughout this entire area and you can certainly pick and chose the route and length of hike that you want. We suggest that you take your time and explore all of it. When we hiked the area we started to the left of the pavilion and went on the outside loop. We decided not to give you a specific route to take but rather to let you discover the nooks and crannies on your own. There are bridges, waterfalls and ponds, ducks and deer, and so many things to learn. Please be respectful of this secret treasure and enjoy.

Deer Run Loop
.4 mile total

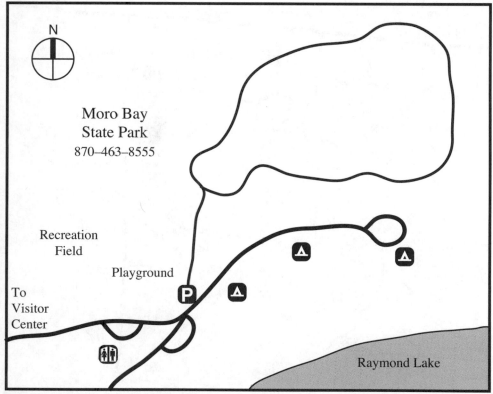

N

Moro Bay
State Park
870–463–8555

Recreation
Field

Playground

To
Visitor
Center

Raymond Lake

Deer Run Loop. Moro Bay State Park is an excellent destination for people who want to get away but not too far away from civilization. The park is located just 30 minutes away from El Dorado or Warren. It has a couple of delightful hikes but one of them (The Low Water Trail) is only open during low water.

To get to Moro Bay State Park from El Dorado off U.S. Hwy. 82, take Hwy. 63 north 22 miles to the park: or, from Warren, travel 30 miles south on Hwy. 63 to the park. Once inside the park you will pass a picnic area on your right and a pavilion on your left, take the next road to the left. This road is just before the Visitor Center. Be sure to stop in and say hi. Follow the road to the playground area and park there. Look across the field and you will see a sign for the Deer Run Trail.

The trail begins directly behind the sign and heads off to the right on a boardwalk. You will hear the sound of traffic along this trail which is just a reminder of how important quiet places are. Other than the traffic noise this is an incredibly beautiful hike. The boardwalk continues off and on throughout this hike meandering through an incredible forest. As you hike along be sure to stop and take in a deep breath of clean pine forest aroma. At .1 mile you will come to an intersection and TURN LEFT. If the boardwalks are wet they may be slippery at times, so watch your step. At .3 mile you will come to an intersection with pine trees in the middle, you can either go left or right it doesn't matter, they both take you back to the parking area.

Periwinkle Loop
1.5 miles total

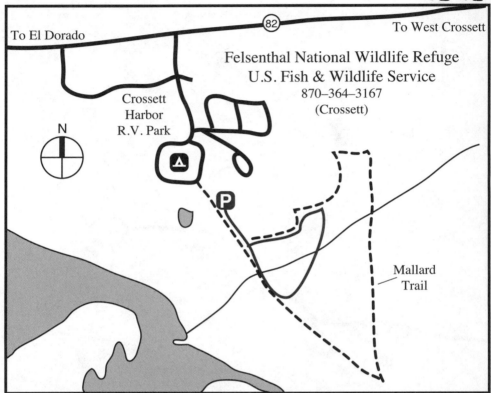

To El Dorado   (82)   To West Crossett

Felsenthal National Wildlife Refuge
U.S. Fish & Wildlife Service
870–364–3167
(Crossett)

Crossett
Harbor
R.V. Park

N

Mallard
Trail

Periwinkle Loop. To get to the Sand Prairie Complex of trails go five miles west of West Crossett on Hwy. 82 and turn into the Crossett Harbor R. V. Park. Go straight ahead past the registration booth and curve around and at 1.1 mile from the highway you will see a Hiking Trail on your right. There is a road that turns to the right and you can park at the trail sign.

There are several trails in this area but we are only going to explore the Periwinkle Trail. Periods of high water may make this trail inaccessible, and during hunting season the trail is closed to hikers. You may want to check with the U.S. Fish and Wildlife Service before hiking this trail. Don't forget the bug spray, you'll need it on this trail. There are interpretive signs along the way and the trail takes out on a wide level path. A beautiful pine forest is the first treat on the trail and at .1 mile you will come to a pond. The trail curves around the edge of the pond and heads into the woods on the other side. Follow the purple blazes. At .2 mile you will come to an intersection—continue STRAIGHT ahead. At .4 mile you will cross a bridge. Right after the bridge there are a couple of roads that come in from the right—stay to the left. The trail comes out into a big open meadow and you will see the purple marker across the way—aim for it. The trail curves to the left here and heads into the woods and under a vine-covered archway. At .7 mile the trail goes slightly downhill and curves to the left, then crosses a bridge. At .9 mile you will come to an intersection, TURN LEFT. Shortly after the intersection you cross another bridge and come to another intersection, TURN LEFT. At 1.1 mile the trail curves to the right. At 1.2 mile you will be back at the original intersection, TURN RIGHT to head back to the parking area.

Delta Woodlands Loop
1.0 mile total

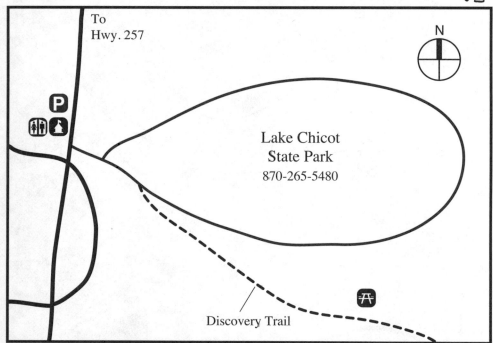

To Hwy. 257

N

P

Lake Chicot
State Park
870-265-5480

Discovery Trail

Delta Woodlands Loop. To get to Lake Chicot State Park take Hwy. 144 from U.S. 65 at Lake Village and drive eight miles northeast to the park; or, take Hwy. 257 from U.S. 65 southeast four miles to Hwy. 144, follow it northeast five miles to the park. There is camping, playground, fishing, and a swimming pool at this State Park. A lot to do! If you have time be sure to drive into the town of Lake Village. The drive by the lake is just beautiful with all of the HUGE Cypress Trees.

The trail begins directly across and behind a little from the Visitor Center, parking is located at the Visitor Center. After hiking into the woods just a little ways you will come to the first intersection. This is a loop trail, continue STRAIGHT ahead. Shortly after the intersection you will see a trail taking off to the right (The Ponds Trail/Discovery Trail), continue STRAIGHT ahead. At .2 mile you will come to a wooden bridge. You are following along an old, level road with huge trees towering above. At .7 mile the trail gently curves to the left and then back to the right. At .8 mile you will pass a bench. This is a great trail for beginner hikers and those making a first trip into the woods. At .9 mile you will be back to the original intersection, TURN RIGHT to go back to the beginning of the trail.

Dragonflies can fly up to 35 mph.

Check for ticks when you are
done hiking a trail.

Delta View Loop
2.5 miles total

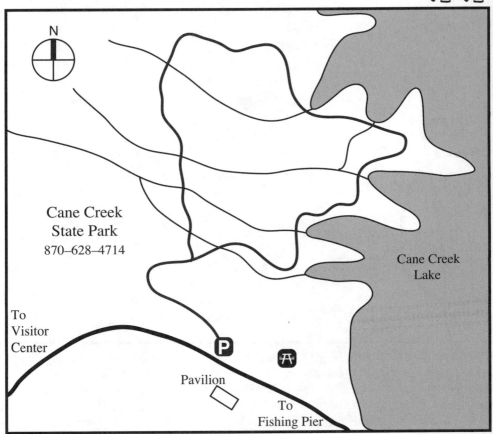

N

Cane Creek
State Park
870–628–4714

Cane Creek
Lake

To
Visitor
Center

P

Pavilion

To
Fishing Pier

Delta View Loop. To get to the Cane Creek State Park from Star City go five miles east on Hwy. 293. Be sure to stop in at the Visitor Center and listen to what a Beaver sounds like. To get to the trailhead continue straight ahead past the Visitor Center. The trail begins across the road from Pavilion #1. There is parking on the left side of the road. Watch for deer because this park is FULL of them. No swimming is allowed at this State Park.

The trail starts out to the left of the Delta View Trail sign and meanders through the woods. There are informational signs along the way. At .5 mile you will come to an intersection, continue STRAIGHT ahead. At .6 mile you will cross a wooden bridge. After the bridge you will head up a slight hill. The trail meanders through the forest and crosses another bridge at .8 mile, be careful, the bridge will be slippery if wet. At 1 mile you will come to a bench on an overlook of Cane Creek Lake. Great spot for a snack but be sure to take your trash with you. Shortly after the bench you will cross another bridge and head up a hill. At 1.3 mile cross another bridge and shortly after that another bridge. The views during leaf-off will be incredible and in the spring the flowering dogwoods and redbuds will take your breath away. At 1.5 mile another bridge and again at 1.6 mile. There will be a couple more bridges after this and then you will arrive back to the intersection where you will TURN RIGHT to get back to the parking area.

Discovery Loop
.5 mile total

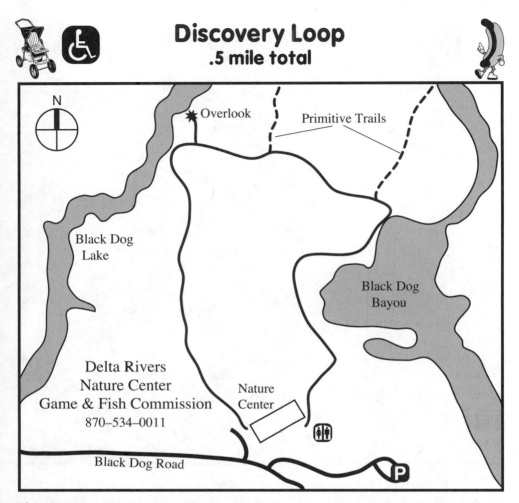

Discovery Loop. A kids' paradise! How is that for an introduction. The Delta River Nature Center is simply amazing, and even if you don't hike the trail the trip is well worth it just to visit the Center. Be sure to check everything out. There are so many hidden treasures to discover. They do have specific hours that they are open but the trail is open all of the time. Off of Hwy. 65 in Pine Bluff turn north on Convention Center Drive and go .9 mile to the entrance of the Delta Rivers Nature Center.

The trail begins to the right behind the restrooms and pavilion on a paved path. The trail curves to the left and comes to a boardwalk. Out to your right is a little lake of sorts. Watch for alligators. There are new trails being built through here, stay on the pavement unless you want to explore a little bit more. There are interpretive signs along the way. There is another boardwalk at .2 mile. After going through a little clearing you will come to another boardwalk at .3 mile. On this boardwalk you will come to an intersection, if you TURN RIGHT you will go to an observation tower. Walk quietly though and look for wildlife. Back at the intersection TURN RIGHT to continue. At the end of this boardwalk be sure to look to your left at a tree called a toothache tree. We didn't know trees had teeth but it sure looks like it is in pain. There are a few more boardwalks to cross and at .5 mile you will be back to the Visitor Center. Before you head in though... as soon as you pass the fence and step into the clearing, look to your right and see the birds of prey.

Old Townsite Loop
1.4 miles total

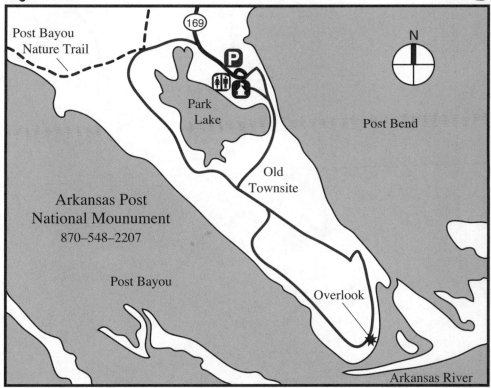

Old Townsite Loop. From Dewitt go south on Hwy. 1/Hwy. 165 to Hwy. 169, turn left and go 2.3 miles to the park. As you drive over the bridges on this highway notice the lotus blooming. And if there are people stopped along the way, most likely they'll be looking at alligators!

Make your way to the Visitor Center and stop in to learn about why this area is so important. Visitor Center hours are 8 to 5 but the trails are open until dark. When you walk out the door of the Visitor Center turn right to begin the trail. There are informational signs along the way.

The first thing you will come to is a cannon looking out over the bayou—the trail TURNS RIGHT. To your left is the Post Bend and it's interesting how the water keeps pushing its way in. At the next intersection TURN LEFT to continue the trail or turn right to go back to the Visitor Center. The Post Bend is to your left and Park Lake is to your right. At .1 mile you will come to another intersection and you will TURN RIGHT. This is called the American Townsite. There is a maze of paths through here that can be explored, however once you have turned right you will walk to the very end of this path.

Once you get to the end of the pavement TURN LEFT. At .3 mile you will see a trail that is paved—head to the RIGHT, and continue STRAIGHT ahead into the woods. You'll cross over a bridge, come to an intersection, and then TURN LEFT. The trail turns to black pavement and TURN RIGHT.

At .6 mile you will come to an intersection, TURN LEFT and go out to the Arkansas River Overlook. When you are looking out at the river, notice how the Lotus plants stop growing where the river meets the Post Bend and the Post Bayou. Return to the trail and TURN LEFT. At .7 mile, you'll cross another bridge. Looking off to your left you will see the Post Bayou. At .9 mile you will come back into the Old Townsite, then TURN LEFT, and continue STRAIGHT ahead into the woods on the other side. At 1.0 mile the trail curves to the left and the Park Lake is on your right. At 1.2 mile you will come to an intersection—continue STRAIGHT ahead to the parking area.

Scavenger Hunt ? Who had the following recipe for removing warts?
"Barley-corn-Barley-corn, injun-meal shorts, Spunk-water, spunk-water, swaller these warts, and then walk away quick, eleven steps, with your eyes shut, and then turn around three times and walk home without speaking to anybody. Because if you speak the charm's busted."

On the day of a full moon it will rise at sundown and go down at sunup.

Frogs are wet and slimy. Toads are dry and warty.

Keep your distance from all snakes unless a grown-up can tell what it is.

The armadillo's response to surprise is to jump three to four feet straight up in the air. Due to this response its most formidable predator is the automobile.

Upland Nature Trail
.7 mile round trip

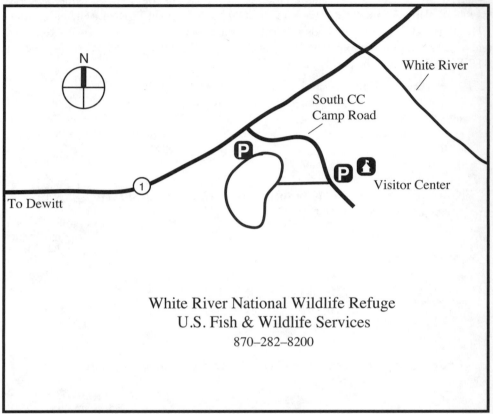

White River

South CC
Camp Road

N

P

P

Visitor Center

1

To Dewitt

White River National Wildlife Refuge
U.S. Fish & Wildlife Services
870–282–8200

Upland Nature Trail. The White River National Wildlife Refuge and visitor center have so many things to offer that many people in the state of Arkansas just don't even realize exist in our wonderful state. The swamp area and farmlands of east Arkansas have a distinct beauty all their own and the White River Wildlife Refuge is a great place to start to learn about this beauty. Be sure to stop in at the Visitor Center to see some great exhibits about how this land was formed and the wildlife that can be found. Outside of the Visitor Center is a great little .7 mile loop trail that is paved and is wheelchair and stroller accessible. From the trailhead parking we head off to the right into the woods and follow the trail as it curves around. There are plenty of informational panels along the way with benches if you need a rest. At .5 mile you will come to a boardwalk bridge with a spur bridge leading off to the right that will take you back to the Visitor Center. Continue straight ahead and you will end the trail back at the parking area.

To get to the White River National Wildlife Refuge Visitor Center turn off of Hwy. 1 onto South CC Camp Road, just outside of St. Charles, Arkansas. You will see the beginning of the Upland Trail just to your right. Just follow the signs.

Scavenger Hunt ? **When was the White River National Wildlife Refuge formed?**

Champion Tree Trail
2.4 mile round trip

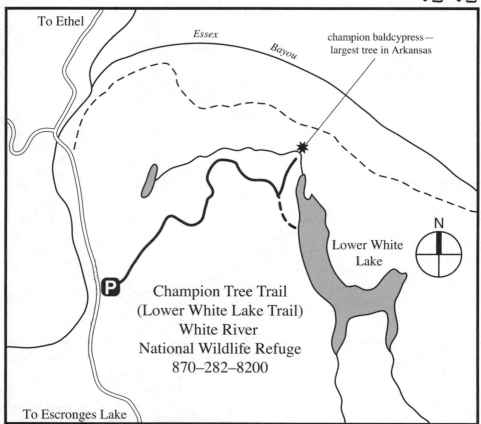

To Ethel

Essex *Bayou*

champion baldcypress—
largest tree in Arkansas

Lower White
Lake

N

P

Champion Tree Trail
(Lower White Lake Trail)
White River
National Wildlife Refuge
870–282–8200

To Escronges Lake

Champion Tree Trail. This trail will lead you to the largest cypress tree in Arkansas. It is a beauty to behold and will shock you that something like this lives in our state. The area is prone to flooding so be sure to check with the Visitor Center to make sure the trail is open. Follow the trail from the trailhead for about one mile then turn left at the trail intersection taking a smaller trail to the tree. Don't forget your camera and bug spray!!

To get to the trailhead from Hwy. 1, turn south on Hwy. 17 and travel to Ethel. Turn left at the Ethel store and follow the paved road to the Refuge entrance. Turn right towards Smokehouse campground. Drive past the Smokehouse campground until you come to a "Y" intersection. Turn left passing over Essex Bayou and travel for about one mile. Trailhead will be on your left.

Louisiana Purchase Boardwalk
.4 mile round trip

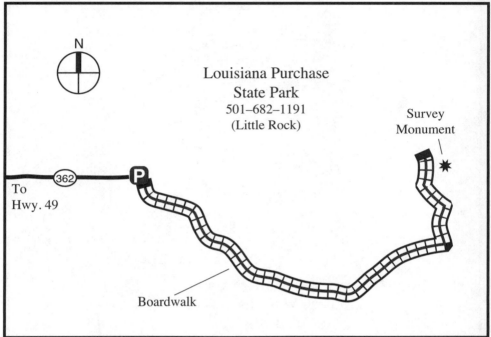

N

Louisiana Purchase
State Park
501–682–1191
(Little Rock)

Survey
Monument

P

362

To
Hwy. 49

Boardwalk

Louisiana Purchase Boardwalk. An amazing trail for those of you who have never been to a swamp before. Very informative, beautiful and kind of eerie. There are no indoor facilities here such as Visitor Center, nor is there camping or anything else really, but it is worth it just to experience this unique trail. To get to the park from I-40 take Hwy. 49 south at Brinkley about 21 miles to Hwy. 362, go east two miles on Hwy. 362 to the park.

The boardwalk trail starts out from the parking area and is filled with interpretive signs along the way. You will be hiking above (and not in, thank goodness) a headwater swamp. This area marks the initial Louisiana Purchase Land Survey and it is a true wonder why they picked this spot. Of course, along this hike you'll learn WHY they did choose this exact location. We won't give it away, go find out for yourself. As you are hiking along be sure to listen closely to the sounds of the life of a swamp. As you look into the black waters of a swamp let your imagination run wild as to the things that live below. Please stay on the boardwalk and do not venture off (who would want to?). Alligators have been spotted here, and you may think that you are hearing the calls of birds but actually that is a bird sounding Frog. Do you see one? This is an in and out trail so after you have enjoyed the headwater swamp return to the parking area the way you came in.

When the buttonbush blooms during the summer, the insects swarm, so be prepared.

Scavenger Hunt ? When the monument was dedicated, were the people
standing in the swamp or were they on dry land?

Bear Creek Loop
1.0 mile total

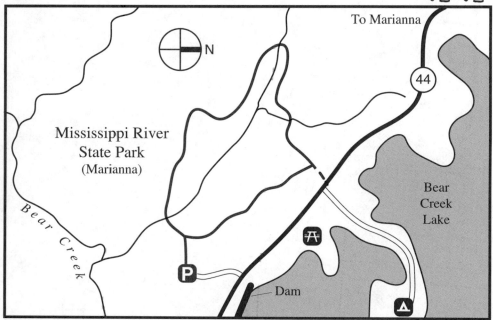

Bear Creek Loop. This is a wonderful trail that winds around past huge trees and lots of giant grape vines. It's out of the way, but worth the effort. Take Hwy. 44 east out of Marianna (a National Scenic Byway) to the Bear Creek Recreation Area. Just before you cross the dam of Bear Creek Lake (opposite the beach), turn to the right and head down the access road to the trailhead. You are in the new Mississippi River State Park, and this area is actually part of Crowley's Ridge (and within the St. Francis National Forest). It's kind of strange to see such forested hillsides here that rise up out of the Mississippi River Delta. There are numerous numbered posts along the trail—these point out the different species of trees that are found along the trail. (A brochure may be available at the new state park visitor center nearby.)

There is a spur trail that goes from the trailhead on down to the trail—TURN RIGHT and follow the trail around to the right, across a bridge, and up the hill. It soon tops out and runs along a narrow ridge—lots of huge trees and vines. At an intersection the main trail TURNS LEFT and runs down another narrow ridgetop (the trail to the right just goes out to the highway). It swings around to the right, and drops down to and across the first of several bridges. It winds around in the bottom to another bridge across the main creek, then eventually swings up into another ravine and climbs the hill. All along the trail you'll see wonderful big trees. At one point the trail goes right between two of the largest.

When the trail tops out it hits an old roadbed and TURNS LEFT, and runs along the top of a narrow ridge for a hundred yards or so. There is a timber cut area on the right that is growing up. This is quite a contrast to the huge trees on the other side. The trail bears to the left, past a bench, and goes along the center of another narrow ridgetop. There are some pretty nice views down into the ravine below. At the end of the ridge there is a set of steps that takes you swiftly down to the bottom again and across two long bridges. Pause for a while here 'cause the end is near. A little ways off of the end of the bridges is the spur trail back to the trailhead. The total distance is about a mile.

Military Road Loop
2.2 miles total

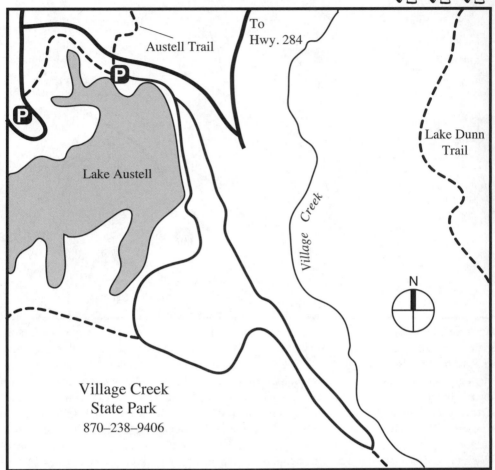

Military Road Loop. This is the first of two trails at this neat park we'll describe here, but there are more to hike and plenty to see and do there. To get to Village Creek State Park take Exit 242 off I-40 just east of Forrest City and travel 13 miles north on Hwy. 284; or travel six miles south on Hwy. 284 from Wynne.

To get to the trailhead from the Visitor Center parking lot turn right and go .7 mile to the Boat Launch Ramp parking area. Walk down the hill toward the lake, you will see a sign on your left, TURN LEFT. The trail immediately crosses a bridge and heads downhill. During leaf-off the views will be spectacular. There are several bridges through here and if it is wet be careful, it will be slippery. At .1 mile the trail comes to the dam, TURN RIGHT and cross the dam. Once you cross the dam at .2 mile the trail curves to the right and comes close to the water. At .3 mile the trail turns to the left and goes up a set of steps. You'll meet an intersection at .4 mile, turn to the left to go to an overlook, turn to the right to continue the hike. At .6 mile you will come to an intersection, TURN LEFT and continue along a wide road. If you hike this trail anytime other than winter, insect repellent is a must. At 1.25 miles you will see a set of steps go up the left side of the embankment, TURN LEFT here. Be watching for this intersection, if you miss it you're in for a long hike. Once you are on the other side of the embankment you will go down a set of steps, curve to the left and be on regular trail. At 1.3 miles the trail curves back to the left, watch for the blazes on the tree. Shortly after this curve you will cross a wooden bridge. Several bridges follow this and the trail meanders through the forest. At 1.5 miles the trail crosses another wooden bridge and then curves sharply back to the left. At 1.7 miles cross a metal bridge and now you are in the bottomlands. At 2.0 miles you will come to a pond/swampy area, watch for HUGE turtles splashing into the water. Continue STRAIGHT across the open area below the dam. Once you get across the open field, there is a trail that heads STRAIGHT into the woods or a trail that goes up the side of the dam. Either one, take your pick they will lead you to the same place. We chose up the side of the dam and once to the top you will be back to the Military Road Trail Sign. Head back the same way that you came in from the parking area.

Big Ben Loop
.5 mile total

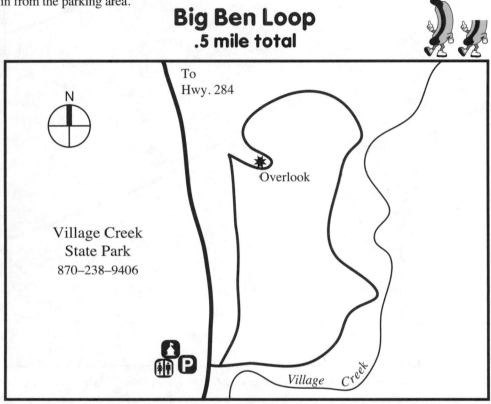

Big Ben Loop. This is the main educational trail for this State Park and is used for many school groups. Along the way you will see the many aspects of Crowley's Ridge. Parking is available at the Visitor Center and the trail takes off across the road. At the sign for the Big Ben Nature Trail go to the right and head down a set of steps. Continue STRAIGHT ahead toward the number post 1. Please stay on the trail. At the Visitor Center you can pick up the brochure that goes along with the numbers. At .1 mile you will come to an overlook of Village Creek, continue STRAIGHT ahead. At .2 mile you will come to another overlook, if the water is running it will be beautiful and it is a great place to stop for a snack. The trail curves back to the left and comes to a wooden bridge. The trail begins the up portion of your adventure and goes through some really neat areas. At .3 mile there is a set of steps and once to the top of the steps it levels out and comes to another overlook with a railing. The trail curves back to the right. Shortly after you will come to a very steep set of steps and once down those steps the trail turns to the left. Follow this old roadbed all the way back to the trailhead.

Dancing Rabbit Loop
1.3 miles total

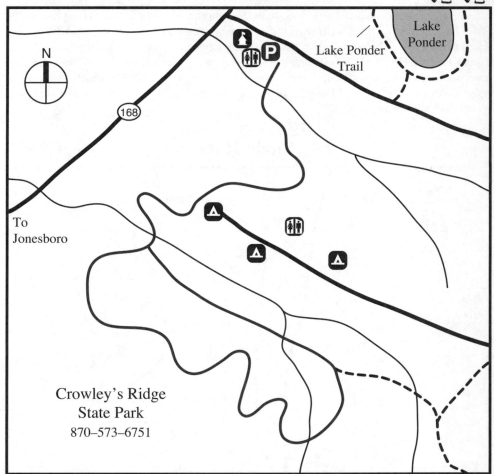

You could spend a week at this State Park and never get it all done. Crowley's Ridge State Park has it all, including one of the neatest swimming areas that we have ever seen. We'll do two of the trails here. To get to the park from Jonesboro travel 15 miles north on Hwy. 141 to Walcott and turn to the right at the Y intersection onto Hwy. 168; or from Paragould follow Hwy. 412 west for 10 miles then go two miles south on Hwy. 168. Turn right (if coming from the south) into the park and park at the Visitor Center.

Dancing Rabbit Loop. The trail begins next to the Visitor Center on the left. First thing you will find is a beautiful swinging bridge. Right after the bridge you will head up a hill and curve to the left. There are a few steep sections on this trail. Not to worry though, they may be steep but they don't last long. At .1 mile you will come to an intersection, continue STRAIGHT ahead. At .2 mile you will see a campground over to your left. The trail curves to the right away from the campground and heads down a slope. At .3 mile you will begin to descend some steps toward the next swinging bridge. Directly AFTER crossing the swinging bridge you will come to an intersection, TURN LEFT. The trail is fairly level through here with a gentle stroll next to a stream. At .4 mile you will cross over the third bridge. At .5 mile you will come to a sign with arrows pointing to the campground or picnic area, CONTINUE STRAIGHT AHEAD. At .6 mile the trail curves to the right and heads downhill, shortly after this you will come to another bridge. After the bridge the trail curves to the left and climbs steeply up a hill. The trail meanders through some huge pine trees and white oaks. Simply stunning. There is some up and downing through here, just take your time. At .8 mile you will begin down a steep hill. Did I mention it was STEEP! There are steps through here so take your time. At .9 mile the trail curves back to the right and you will see the swinging bridge and an intersection, TURN LEFT. Unless of course, you want to do the trail again. You are now on the trail that you came in on. Follow the trail back to the parking area.

Scavenger Hunt ? Did you see any dancing rabbits?

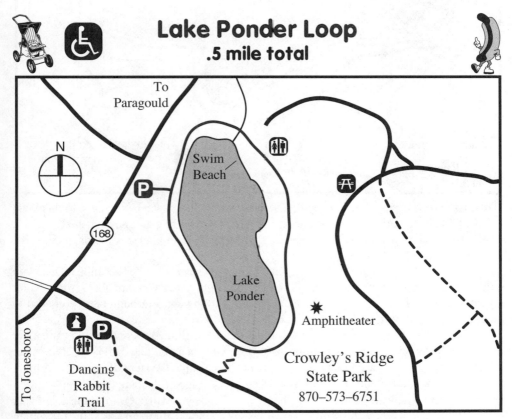

Lake Ponder Loop
.5 mile total

Lake Ponder Loop. This is a paved, barrier-free trail that is perfect for strollers and wheel-chairs. The main parking area is right along the highway next to the lake. If you need access to the barrier free parking travel through the State Park curving to the left to the parking area there.

There is a swim beach, paddleboat dock, playground, snack bar and much more at this trail. It may be crowded at times, but well worth the visit. Follow the paved trail, remaining close to the lake at all times. This is a loop trail and you should be able to see the parking area the entire hike. Beware though, you may go there for a short hike and wind up spending the day. So much to do!!!!!

131

Trappers Lake Loop
.9 mile total

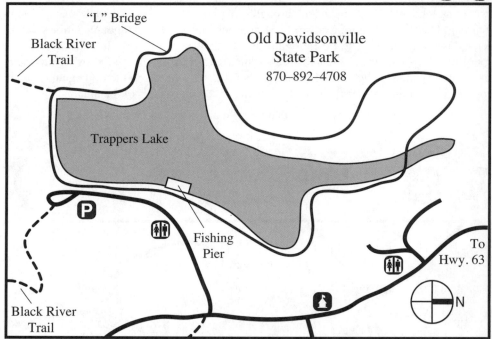

"L" Bridge

Black River
Trail

Old Davidsonville
State Park
870–892–4708

Trappers Lake

P

Fishing
Pier

To
Hwy. 63

N

Black River
Trail

Trappers Lake Loop. What a neat little surprise you will find when you come to this State Park. FULL of historical value of one of the first towns in this area, established in 1815. There is no swimming allowed in Trappers Lake. There is camping, restrooms, picnic area a playground, and catfish fishing!

From U.S. Hwy. 63 at Black Rock, take State Hwy. 361 north for six miles. Once you pull into the park the Visitor Center will be on your right. After you pass the Visitor Center take the next road on your right. There are several parking areas through here, you need to go to the very end of the drive where there is a circle drive, park here.

At the end of the circle drive you will see a sign for a hiking trail and limit 5 catfish per day. We will start out heading across the dam. Once you get across the dam you will come to an intersection, there is a sign that says Trappers Lake Trail to the right. If the water is high, the trail will be impassable. The trail follows along the edge of the lake (reminder—limit 5 catfish per day). There are benches along the way. At .2 mile you will come to a little boardwalk that goes out over the lake. At .4 mile you will begin a gradual climb up a hill but still remain by the lake. At .5 mile you will come to a line of GIANT oak trees. Just past the giant oak trees there is a sign that says DANGER: KEEP OUT. Turn to the right here and head down the hill. At .6 mile you will cross a bridge back over the lake, you will be heading toward the playground. Directly after you cross the lake turn to the right and cross over a smaller bridge. Once past the smaller bridge head up the hill to the paved sidewalk. The sidewalk follows along the edge of the lake and this portion of the trail is stroller and wheelchair accessible. At .8 mile you will arrive at the fishing pier, continue STRAIGHT ahead to the parking area.

And once again don't forget....only 5 catfish per day.

Black River Loop
1.1 miles total

Old Davidsonville
State Park
870–892–4708

N

Trappers Lake Loop

Trappers
Lake

Fishing
Pier

P

Historic
Town Site

Black
River

To
Visitor
Center

Black River Loop. Here is the second trail we'll hike in this neat park, and in fact both trails begin at the same parking area so you can do them both at the same time.

From this circle drive you will begin hiking across the dam. Once across the dam there is a sign for Trappers Lake Trail to the right, we will TURN LEFT. At .1 mile you will head into the woods and curve to the right. After curving back to the left the trail levels out and is a gentle stroll through the woods. At .3 mile you will come to Reeves Cemetery and you will turn toward the right. At .4 mile you will go down a small embankment and cross a bridge. At .5 mile the trail curves to the left and the stream that you have been following empties into the Black River (although it looked kind of brown to us). There are some neat cypress trees through here. At .6 mile cross another bridge. At .7 mile the trail leaves the river and curves to the left, shortly thereafter the trail comes out onto a mowed path. The path widens and then opens up at .8 mile. Notice the HUGE oak tree. This is the old town site of Davidsonville, and site of the FIRST courthouse and post office in Arkansas. Walk up to the paved road and TURN LEFT. Walk along the road and learn about the history of the area through the posted signs. Continue STRAIGHT ahead on this road and at 1.0 mile you will see a sign on your left marking a trail. Take off into the woods and this path will take you directly back to your car.

Wear long pants to hike, even in summer,
it helps keep bugs off and stickers out.

Butterflies & Blooms Trail
.3 mile round trip

White Oak Loop
.9 mile total

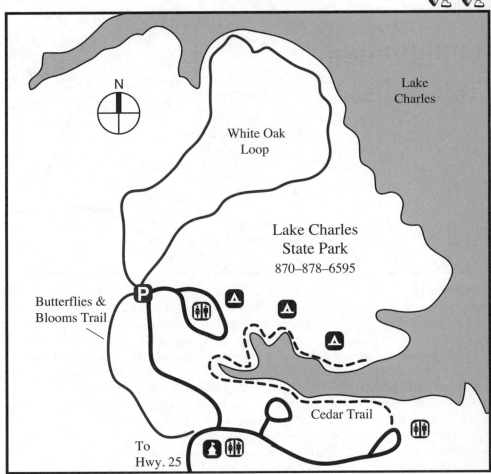

Lots of folks camp and fish at this park, but most never get to hike the trails. To get to Lake Charles State Park from U.S. Hwy. 63 go north on Hwy. 25. This is a strange little loop turn so watch for the signs. (You will leave Hwy. 63 and then take a sharp turn to the right and go under Hwy. 63.) It is almost six miles south on Hwy. 25 to the entrance of the park on the right. The Visitor Center is on your right, be sure to stop in and see what wonderful programs they have planned for the day. Take the next left, drop down the hill and park just past the dump station. There is parking on the left and restrooms to the right.

Butterflies & Blooms Trail. Here is an easy trail with a hard packed surface. Heavy duty jogger strollers will be able to make this hike, however wheelchairs will sink in the gravel. It meanders through wildflowers that have been planted on both sides of the trail. Plenty of activity through here in the summer months.

From the parking area take off to the left. There are signs there. Follow the hard packed surface. It curves to the left, drops down the hill and works its way back up again toward the Visitor Center. This is not a loop trail, but can be made into one by following the road back (watch for traffic though). This is a perfect outing for those really little ones that need to stretch their legs or for the young at heart, but older in body, that love being out enjoying the flowers, but are not looking for a strenuous hike.

White Oak Loop. This loop trail begins at the same parking area as the first one. It heads off the opposite direction out into the deep woods, then drops down and runs along the lake shore. There are some nice views when the leaves are off. Be sure to save some energy for the return loop, which is mostly uphill.

From the parking area head off to the woods to the right. There is a food plot straight ahead but stay to the RIGHT. The trail is fairly level and wanders through some huge hardwood trees. If you are here in the springtime you might get to see buckeye trees in bloom with their bright red flowers.

The trail is a little up and downing and eventually drops down the hill and comes to the edge of the lake at a bench at .4 mile. This is a great place for a snack. After the bench the trail curves to the left and follows along the lake shore. Very nice easy walking through here. At about .8 mile the trail curves to the left and starts up a hill. You will be leaving the lake shore at this point. There is a wide open field with a tall fence on your right at about 1.1 mile. There is an intersection at 1.2 mile, TURN LEFT here to return to your car.

 If you stop to tie your shoe, tie the other one too.

 Have a hiking buddy.

Raccoons often take their food to a nearby stream or pond to wash it carefully before eating it.

Tunstall River Walk
1.3 miles round trip

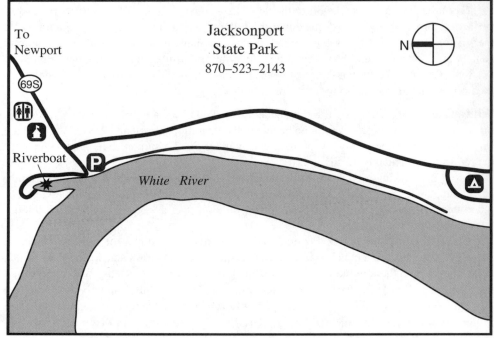

Tunstall River Walk. Traveling north on Hwy. 67 into Newport take exit 83 and turn left (west) on Hwy. 384 and travel one mile to Hwy. 367. Turn left (south) onto Hwy. 367 and travel two miles to Hwy. 69 and turn right (north). Travel Hwy. 69 three miles to Jacksonport. Pass the Visitor Center and come to a stop sign, continue straight ahead and parking will be to your left. There is a riverboat tour located at this State Park and plenty of historical things to learn about. There are fees to tour the river boat and the old courthouse. Bug spray is a must on this trail.

The trail takes off across the levee on flat level ground, and it may be possible to get a jogger stroller through here. There are benches across the way with views of the White River. Huge cottonwoods and wildflowers line the path. At .6 mile you will reach the edge of the campground, turn around and head back the same way you came in.

Scavenger Hunt ❓ What is the name of the riverboat?

Do not pick the flowers or the chiggers will pick you.

Dragonflies eat other insects, including mosquitoes.

Knapp Loop
.8 mile total

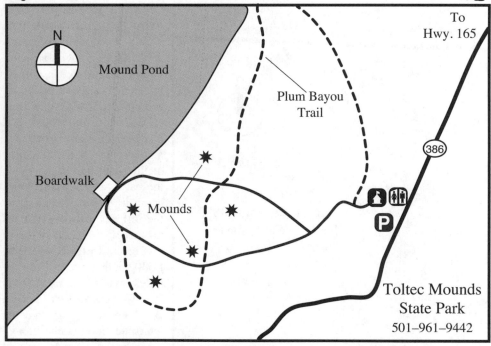

To
Hwy. 165

N

Mound Pond

Plum Bayou
Trail

386

Boardwalk

Mounds

P

Toltec Mounds
State Park
501–961–9442

Knapp Loop. Toltec Mounds is located close to Little Rock and is a great educational experience. To get there from I-440 take Exit 7, going southeast on Hwy. 165 for nine miles to the park. To enter this trail you must go through the Visitor Center (there is a small fee). We suggest you take a look at the museum first, things will make much more sense when you get out into the mounds area. This State Park is on limited hours and the trails are closed to the public when the State Park is not open. THEY ARE CLOSED ON MONDAYS. You may want to call first to check their schedule.

The Knapp Trail is an interpretive trail so be sure to pick up a brochure before you head out. You will head out of the Visitor Center on a paved path. Be sure to STAY OFF OF THE MOUNDS. As you head out into the open area the Knapp Trail takes off to your left staying on pavement the whole time (except for the boardwalk). The entire trail is flat and easy. There are benches and shelters along the way and if you hike this in the summer take advantage of those areas to cool down. Take plenty of water. At the first, second and third intersections continue STRAIGHT ahead staying on payment. The third intersection that takes off to your right is paved as well but continue STRAIGHT ahead to the boardwalk. As you head into the woods on the boardwalk you will go behind mound A, be careful, the boardwalk will be slippery when wet. Spectacular spot through here with the cypress trees and an overlook out into Mound Pond. Watch for turtles and other critters. The boardwalk curves around to the right and the trail heads STRAIGHT back to the Visitor Center.

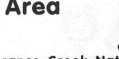

Lorance Creek Natural Area
.5 mile round trip

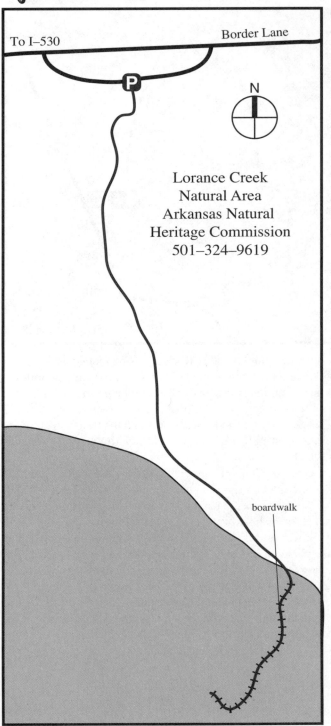

To I–530

Border Lane

P

N

Lorance Creek
Natural Area
Arkansas Natural
Heritage Commission
501–324–9619

boardwalk

Lorance Creek Natural Area is a small scenic area with a paved trail and boardwalk that goes out into a dense swamp. It is located just off the interstate between Little Rock and Pine Bluff and is quick and easy to get to and to hike, and is wheelchair accessible. It's a great place to visit any time of the year, but especially in the early spring when things begin to bloom, and again in the fall when the hardwoods turn color.

From Little Rock, take I-530 south approximately 10 miles, exit at Bingham Road (Exit 9). TURN LEFT (east) on Bingham Road, cross over the interstate, and continue through a residential area. At the first "Y" in the road, go RIGHT on Bingham Road. At the second "Y" in the road, bear RIGHT on Border Lane and the Lorance Creek parking lot is a couple hundred yards on the right. Take the paved trail down into the woods and it will lead to the boardwalk into the swamp.

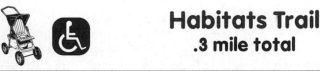

Habitats Trail
.3 mile total

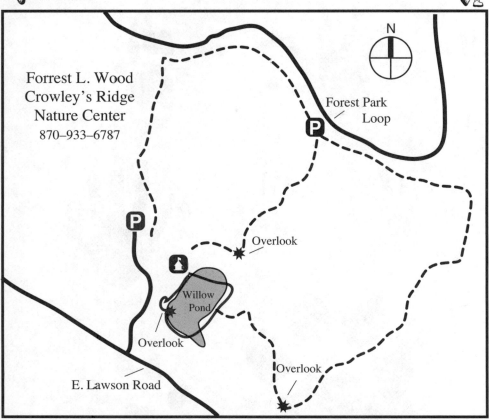

Forrest L. Wood
Crowley's Ridge
Nature Center
870–933–6787

N

Forest Park
Loop

P

P

Overlook

Willow
Pond

Overlook

Overlook

E. Lawson Road

Habitats Trail. What a fantastic nature center located in Jonesboro, filled with so many exhibits and learning experiences for everyone of all ages. Be sure to go into the Wood Crowley's Ridge Nature Center and take a look around. Don't forget to head downstairs and teach the kids what various snakes look like. The Habitats Trail begins out the back side of the nature center and follows along a boardwalk surrounding Willow Pond. There are interpretative signs along the way. Learn what different frogs sound like and be sure to watch for turtles. Be patient and quiet and watch the turtles appear from the depths of the water, just like magic. Once you leave the nature center out the back door, head to the left and follow the boardwalk. As the trail curves around you will see various side trails taking off. All of these trails interconnect and loop around so feel free to make your hike longer. Staying on the main boardwalk, which does turn to pavement for a ways, the Habitats trail makes a complete loop and returns directly to the Nature Center.

The center is located in Jonesboro between Hwy. 1 and S. Culberhouse Road. Take Hwy 1 south from US 63, turn right onto Lawson Road, and then turn into the entrance about 1.5 miles ahead on the right. The center is closed on Mondays but the trails are open from dawn to dusk.

Mammal Tracks

Beaver

Skunk

Chipmunk

Squirrel

Raccoon

Cougar

Bobcat

Wolf

Coyote

Fox

Deer

Armadillo

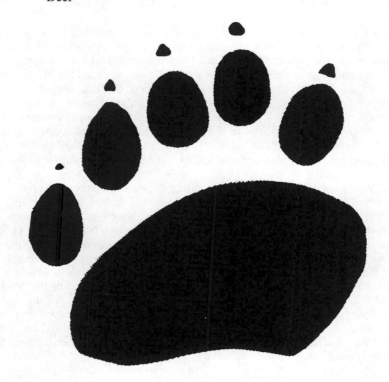

Black bear

Rabbit

Opossum

About the Authors

We are a true hiking family, and live in a log cabin at the edge of the Buffalo River Wilderness in northwest Arkansas. We hike nearly every day of the year, rain or snow or shine, on one of the nearby trails, or right out the front door of the cabin. When I first laid eyes on my future bride, Pam, she was standing at a trailhead getting ready to go hiking—I knew that I had met my match. It has been all downhill ever since, and uphill, and across wildflower-studded meadows in the Rockies, along streams and blufflines in every corner of Arkansas, and everywhere else there is even a hint of a trail—gosh, I'm just trying to keep up, and loving it. Our daughter, Amber, enjoys "bushwhacking" through the dense forest, making her own path, and discovering all there is to see. She is the brains of the outfit, and often makes us stop and examine some tiny detail along the way, leading to questions and discussions about much larger things in life. Our dogs, Wilson and Mia, go with us most of the time. You can read about our life both on and off of the trail at **www. TimErnst.com** *where I keep a daily log of life in the online Little Bluff Journal.*

...T.E.

Pam Ernst, grew up in Nixa, Missouri, a small town just outside of Springfield. While in the middle of an accounting career, she began to make frequent trips down into the Ozarks where she discovered the joys of hiking. Already an accomplished rock climber, hiking allowed her to visit and explore many new places. One of those trips led her to a trail by a lake in Arkansas, where she met her future husband (and married on the same spot the next year). She had always enjoyed writing, and with so many new trails all around her new home, she decided to produce this guidebook to help other moms find their own adventures (dads, and grandparents too!). She has also written a couple of children's books, and will see them published in the near future. And she is quickly becoming an accomplished artist, her pencil sketches and pastels capturing a unique mood and feel of the world around her (she her work at www.PamsPastels.com).

Amber Ernst moved into the wilderness when she was just seven, and has taken to it like a baby bobcat bounces out into the wide-open forest. Like her mom, she also loves to rock climb, and seems to have no fear at all. She also enjoys sports, and has played soccer since she was four, and recently has taken up basketball. Her mind races as fast as her body, and she is enrolled in the Gifted Students program at her small school in Jasper (the bus ride from the cabin to school is more than an hour each way!). She was responsible for going ahead of her mom and pushing the "wheelie" for the trails in this book (a device we use to get accurate distances), calling out the measurements as Pam was recording the details along the way. She kept a log of tips she felt like other kids should know ("Catch the Buzz" from the bee), and also spent a great deal of time pouring through all sorts of books to compile many of the "Wise Old Owl" sayings here. Over the years Amber has hiked on out into the big world beyond wilderness and has become a CPA—she still hikes and explores the great outdoors as often as she can.

Tim Ernst, a native of Fayetteville, Arkansas, has been hiking and exploring the wilderness since he was seven and his dad first took him hunting. He has managed to carve out a living there, with a trio of careers that include nature photography (published in many of the big publications from *National Geographic* on down, has at least 19 coffee-table picture books to his credit, teaches digital photo workshops, and has a complete fine art printing facility at their art gallery near the greater Ponca/Jasper Metroplex); has written dozens of hiking trail guidebooks and distributes them through his publishing business; and has designed and built many hiking trails all over the state, both as a volunteer and contractor. He built a log cabin called Cloudland in 1997, and later found true happiness when he met his life mate and woman of his dreams on a nearby trail. (We recently built a new wilderness cabin hideaway and gallery called Little Bluff that is located near Jasper, but is still isolated.) While he has blazed many trails in his life, and has more books to write and photos to take, he looks forward to following in the footprints of both his wife and daughter and sharing in all the discoveries they will be making.

Notes:

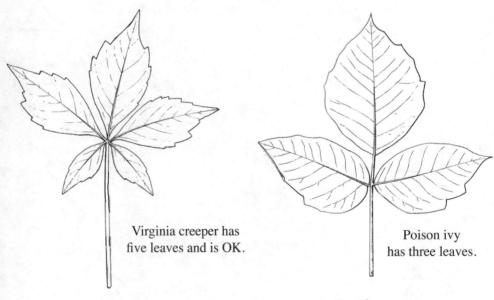

Virginia creeper has
five leaves and is OK.

Poison ivy
has three leaves.

One final word of wisdom—
Leaves Of Three, Let It Be!

Legend For All Maps

———————	Main Trail, described route	**P**	Trailhead Parking
– – – – –	Main Trail, additional route	**P**	Other parking
- - - - -	Other Trails	🚹	Visitor Center
≈≈≈	Creek, Streams, Rivers	🚻	Restroom
||////	Bluffline or Rock Outcrop	▲ ⛱	Campground, Picnic Area
▬▬▬▬	Paved Road	✳	Point of Interest
═══════	Gravel Road	†	Cemetery
= = = = :	Jeep Road	71	Paved Highway
● ■	COMMUNITY/City, Building	23 341	State/County Road-Paved/Gravel
∩ ⋎	Spring, Cave	1003	Gravel Forest Road

31 90 Eureka Spgs. 22 20 12 4 5 93 30

94 29 95 13 11 33 26 7 Mtn. Home Hardy 73 87

Fayetteville 27 23 Harrison 15 89 74 81 75

3 8 14 18 21 32 Jasper 9 6 24 103 Jonesboro

19 10 17 1 92 Mtn. View

34 96 **OZARKS** 91 88 Newport

16 25 Heber Spgs.

Ft. Smith 97 38 39 43 Russellville 83 72

44 99 46 47 36 45 Forrest City

RIVER VALLEY 41 40 37 71

56 57 69 42 98 82

58 35 ★ Little Rock

66 62 53 80 **EAST**

63 54 65 Hot Springs 55 104

Mena 61 59 105 102

48 49 60 68 79

100 52 64 Arkadelphia Pine Bluff 84

101 77

SOUTHWEST

70 67 50 **See back cover for a listing of trails by number**

Texarkana 51 76 78

Magnolia 86 85

El Dorado

144